D A I L Y
MEDITATIONS

Translated from the French
Original title: « Pensées Quotidiennes 2024 »

Front cover: © Larysa Pashkevich/iStock

Original edition:
© 2023, Éditions Prosveta S.A., ISBN 978-2-8184-0539-0

Prosveta S.A – 83600 Fréjus (France)
ISBN 978-2-8184-0540-6
Digital edition : ISBN 978-2-8184-0604-5

Omraam Mikhaël Aïvanhov

D A I L Y
MEDITATIONS

2024

PROSVETA

Foreword

Every morning, before you do anything else, you must give yourself a few quiet moments of reflection so as to begin your day in peace and harmony, and unite yourself to the Creator by dedicating the new day to Him through prayer, meditation.

It is the beginning that is all-important, for it is then, at the beginning, that new forces are set in motion and given direction. If we want to act wisely and well, we have to begin by casting some light on the situation. You do not look for something or start work in the dark; you start by lighting a lamp so that you can see what you are doing. And you can apply the same principle to every area in life: in order to know what to do and how to do it, you have to switch on the light – in other words, to con-centrate and look into yourself. Without this light you will wander in all directions and knock on many different doors, and you will never achieve anything worthwhile.

Our days follow the direction that we give to our first thoughts in the morning, for, depending on whether we are mindful or not, we either clear the way ahead or litter it with all kinds of useless and even dangerous debris. Disciples of initiatic science know how to begin the day so that it may be fruitful and rich in God's grace, and so that they may share that grace with those around them. They understand how important it is to begin the day with one fundamental thought around which all the other thoughts of the day may revolve.

If you keep your sights fixed on a definite goal, a clear orientation, an ideal, all your activities will gradually organize themselves and fall into line in such a way as to contribute to the realization of that ideal. Even the negative or alien thoughts or feelings that attempt to infiltrate you will be deflected and put at the service of the divine world. Yes, even they will be forced to follow the direction you have chosen. In this way, thanks to the fundamental thought that you place in your head and your heart first thing in the morning, your whole day will be recorded in the book of life.

And, since everything we do is recorded, once you have lived one glorious day, one day of eternal life, not only will that day be recorded, not only will it never die, but it will endeavor to get the days that follow to imitate it. Try to live just one day as well as you possibly can, therefore, and it will influence all your days: it will persuade them to listen to its testimony and follow its example, so as to be well balanced, orderly, and harmonious.

Omraam Mikhaël Aïvanhov

Between 1938 and 1985, Omraam Mikhaël Aïvanhov elaborated a spiritual teaching in almost five thousand improvised talks. His words have been preserved in their entirety, as the talks given between 1938 and the early 1960s were taken down in shorthand, and the later ones were recorded on tape and latterly on video.

Many of these recordings have been published in book form by Prosveta, providing a comprehensive guide to the teaching.

GLOSSARY

Definitions of terms as used by the Master Omraam Mikhaël Aïvanhov:

Brotherhood: a collectivity governed by a truly cohesive spirit, in which each individual works consciously for the good of all. (Daily Meditations 2007: 24 February) A brotherhood is a collectivity whose members share the common bond of a broad, luminous consciousness and work with and for each other, and more than that, they work for the whole world. True brotherhood is universal.

Caduceus: the two snakes represent the two currents, positive and negative, of astral light known traditionally as Od and Ob. The one is luminous and hot, the other is dark and cold; one is white, the other black. (Izvor 237 ch. 9)

Collectivity [human]: a group of people, usually quite extensive, united by a common interest, a common organization or common sentiments, or living in the same place or country. (Prosveta, France, provided it)

Collectivity [cosmic]: the totality of beings in the universe, both visible and invisible.

Disinterestedness: refers not to a lack of interest but to an altruism, an absence of bias motivated by interest or advantage. This is a central part of the Master's philosophy. (A New Dawn, part 2, p.120)

Entities: disincarnate beings, drawn to humans and to nature. They may be either light or dark beings, depending on the quality of the vibrations of the person or place attracting them.

Higher Self, Lower Self: must be understood within the context of the Master's teaching concerning the two natures in human beings, the human lower self and the divine higher self, which he calls respectively personality and individuality. (Love and Sexuality, part 2, p. 42)

Impersonal: refers not to a coldness of attitude but to the absence of referral to self.

Individuality: see 'higher self, lower self'.

Personality: see 'higher self, lower self'.

Psychic: (adjective – as in 'psychic life / world / bodies, etc.'): refers not to mediumship but to a human being's subtle energy beyond the physical, i.e. heart and mind (and soul, or soul and spirit, according to the context).

The Rock: a platform at the top of a hill near the Bonfin, where the Master and his disciples gathered every morning, in spring and summer, to meditate and watch the sun rise.

1 January

In this New Year, I wish that all heaven's blessings pour down upon you. May your body be fit, healthy and filled with strength; may your heart bathe in an ocean of pure joy and spiritual contentment; may your intellect be illuminated and shed true light on the whole of your existence. May your soul be a conductor of divine love, and may your spirit feel completely free from all human constraints and prisons.

May you be linked to the great hierarchy of spiritual beings, so that you may work with them to establish the kingdom of God on earth.

Finally, may you overcome every obstacle that stands in your way, so that your spirit rejoices and glorifies the Creator.*

* Related reading: *The New Year,* Brochure No. 301.

2 January

When you experience moments of peace, joy or wonder, take at least a few minutes to share something of these privileged states by way of your thoughts. Think of all the people in the world who are in anguish and despair. Focus your thoughts on them and say, 'Dear brothers and sisters throughout the world, what I have here is so beautiful and luminous that I want to share it with you. Receive some of this beauty, take some of this light!'

As you know, your inner states generate waves that spread out into space, so do not keep your happiness to yourself, share it with others. This way, not only will you be doing them good, but you will also be amplifying your own inner states. Yes, this is a magical phenomenon: in order to hold on to your joy, you must learn to share it.*

* Related reading: *Hrani Yoga – The Alchemical and Magical Meaning of Nutrition,* Complete Works Vol. 16, Chap. IX, Part II.

3 January

Get into the habit of focusing on the summit, that highest point from which you can see the truth about beings and things. Of course, the distance between you and this summit is immense, insurmountable even, and only those who truly live a pure and holy life can hope to reach the topmost peak.*

But each of us can strive to attain it by means of thought, for thought is like a rope that you throw high above you to the point you want to reach, and once the rope holds fast, you can climb. This is what mountaineers do: they throw a rope and they climb up. Yes, you see, you must learn to find these parallels between the physical world and the spiritual world.

* Related reading: *The Powers of Thought,* Izvor No. 224, Chap. 13.

4 January

*S*o many musicians and poets have dreamed of possessing the lyre of Orpheus in order to hold nature and humans under their spell! In reality, the lyre of Orpheus is not a musical instrument, but a symbol of man himself. The seven strings represent the seven bodies: physical, etheric, astral, mental, causal, Buddhic and atmic. Each string has its own vibration and puts us in communication with specific regions of the visible and invisible worlds and their inhabitants.

Most human beings are content to make only one of their strings vibrate – their physical body. They do not bother much with the other strings, which is why they produce nothing but squeaks. Disciples of an initiatic school study the nature and properties of each string, each body, and work to develop them. These exercises involve the whole of one's being; they therefore necessitate a new way of living that takes conscious account of the slightest acts of daily life, for their aim is to achieve a state where there is no longer any dissonance between the physical body, the heart, mind, will, soul and spirit. Those who understand the profound symbolism of the seven-stringed lyre will themselves become lyres vibrating in unison with the entire cosmos, and they will be received among the children of heaven.

5 January

*T*here are times when you feel overwhelmed by the sense that nothing is going right for you. But remember that nowhere is it written that you must be irrevocably crushed by fate. Only those who forget that the spirit lives within them are subject to unrelenting fate. So, whatever trials you must go through, tell yourself, 'I am a spirit and I can change my destiny.'

Of course, you will not be able to change very much to begin with and you may shift from your primitive state by only a hundredth of a degree. But if you continue to work in the same direction, one day, there will be a whole solar system between you and fate. The important thing is to be able to rediscover the power of the spirit that is within you.*

* Related reading: *The Powers of Thought,* Izvor No. 224, Chap. 7.

6 January

*T*he secret of self-mastery lies in a very simple rule: do not allow certain thoughts and feelings to take hold in your head or your heart, for it is then too late to stop their effects. It is relatively easy to replace one thought with another; it is more difficult to replace one feeling with another; and to replace one kind of act with another is more difficult still.

This is because the further we descend into matter, the deeper we sink into the realm of instincts and habits, which are second nature to us. It is easier to change our scientific, philosophical or religious opinions (we sometimes change them in a heartbeat) than to change our hatred, love, affection or desires. And it is even harder to change our habits, which are deeply entrenched in matter. If you are to gain mastery over your actions, you must begin by gaining mastery over your thoughts.*

* Related reading: *The Powers of Thought,* Izvor No. 224, Chap. 4.

7 January

Celestial entities love the light, and when they catch sight of someone who is surrounded by this light that Initiatic Science calls the aura, they rush towards them.

So, you have years of work to do on yourselves in order to attract all that is truly beautiful and beneficial in the universe. If I ask you, 'Do you truly care about your health, beauty, peace and happiness? Do you truly want to be loved?' you will all reply, 'Yes, yes that is all that matters to us!' Well then, why aren't you doing anything to get it? These blessings cannot come to you simply by chance. The best way to attract them is to work on your aura: vivify it with your love, make it more luminous with your wisdom, make it powerful with your strength of character, and make it bright and clear by leading a pure life. Those who patiently and sincerely devote themselves to the practice of the virtues gradually acquire an immense aura. Not only do celestial creatures come to bathe in it, so do human beings who feel nourished, soothed, strengthened and transported in a divine direction.*

* Related reading: *Man's Subtle Bodies and Centres,* Izvor No. 219, Chap. 2.

8 January

We must renew our efforts to improve ourselves every day. Even if we do not always succeed, the fact that we try will vindicate us in the eyes of heaven. Heaven will never blame us for not succeeding; it is our efforts that count, and our efforts depend on us.

When heaven sees that despite all the obstacles, we continue on our path without faltering, it ordains that our task shall be made lighter. Then joy, light, beauty and freedom will pour down on us. The gifts we receive will be chosen to suit our character, our structure, our affinities, the work we are called on to do, and whatever we need for our evolution.*

* Related reading: *The Zodiac, Key to Man and to the Universe,* Izvor No. 220, Chap. 10.

9 January

When the first man dwelt in close and constant communion with the Lord, nothing was hidden from him.* The divine life in which he was immersed was his unique and perfect source of knowledge. To know something is to taste it. If you want to recover something of that primordial knowledge, you must commune with the universe, with the ocean of cosmic light.

Until you are able to rise to the level of consciousness known as 'communion', you cannot taste reality and, consequently, cannot know it. People devise theories and hypotheses that sometimes come close to the truth, but they are never quite right. 'So what is the point of explanations?' you may ask. To stimulate your curiosity, to trigger a desire to experiment and make certain efforts that will enable you finally to experience other states.

* Related reading: *'In Spirit and in Truth'*, Izvor No. 235, Chap. 11.

10 January

*T*ry to remain silent; let silence penetrate your being. Then, your unfettered mind will become capable of the most luminous creations. It is the little things that surge up from below that hinder our powers of thought: the worries, sorrows, grudges and all the prosaic cares of everyday life.

Only by freeing your mind will you be able to build a high ideal within yourself, and continually embellish, strengthen, amplify, intensify and divinize it, adding to it a purer, more beautiful and altruistic element every day. For an ideal is a real, powerful living being that dwells in heavenly realms, and from its dwelling place on high, it watches over you and keeps you from straying. It protects, instructs and inspires you.*

* Related reading: *The Path of Silence,* Izvor No. 229, Chap. 1.

11 January

*O*nce you have understood the worth and the beauty of initiatic teaching, and have made up your mind to embrace it, do not go back on your decision on the pretext that some aspect of it escapes you, or seems too difficult to put into practice. Once you understand that this teaching can give you the methods you need to perfect yourself, to flourish and to live the new life, never abandon it for any reason.

Of course, if your goals and desires are different, you are free. There are other paths, hundreds of them, but they lead in different directions and give you different results, and you are free to choose among them. But if your aim is universal brotherhood and the kingdom of God, you must make everything converge towards this goal of light, joy and love. All the methods of Initiatic Science correspond ideally to this goal.*

* Related reading: *'In Spirit and in Truth'*, Izvor No. 235, Chap. 6.

12 January

*E*ven if your daily life is full of things that distress you, even if you are often jostled and mistreated, it is always possible to cling to or restore a divine state of higher consciousness.* It is simply a habit, a light that has to be acquired: that of living in a state of vigilance, of constant attention to the divine world, of reminding yourself first thing in the morning to keep your thoughts focused on heaven while performing all the ordinary actions of your everyday life.

If you get into the habit of maintaining this attitude throughout the day, you will see that nothing can leave you shaken for long. Bad news, an illness or an accident can be very upsetting, but if you make a habit of keeping your thoughts focused on the divine world, you will overcome difficulties of this kind much more quickly, for God has given all power to the spirit.

* Related reading: *Love and Sexuality (Part II),* Complete Works Vol. 15, Chap. XV.

13 January

*T*he number of different facts and ph
nomena that exist is incalculable. These facts
are governed by laws, which are far fewer in
number, and laws are governed, in turn, by a
few principles, which combine into one unique
principle: God himself. The world of facts is the
world of multiplicity and dispersion, whereas
the divine world is the world of unity. This very
simple key can give you the solution to every
problem.

When people complain that they feel lost in
darkness and chaos, it is simply that they know
nothing of these three worlds – the world of
principles, the world of laws and the world of
facts – and their structure. If they always confine
themselves to the physical, material world, that
is, to facts and events, they will never be able
to see clearly or be in control of the situation.
In order to have a clear vision of things, and
even to act correctly, they must rise by means
of thought to the higher realm of principles in
which the spirit rules, in which reigns the light
of God.*

* Related reading: *The Symbolic Language of Geometrical
Figures,* Izvor No. 218, Chap. 5.

u sense that you have found a ..t is true, try to follow it without anyone's opinion. If you absolutely want to ask questions, ask them of your own soul, your spirit or the God within. You will object that you have never had any answers from them. Well, you are mistaken; when you question the divine principle within you, you always receive an answer. If you fail to hear the answer, it is because the walls of your consciousness are too thick. Make the walls of your consciousness thinner, and you will see that you receive an answer every time.

When you need guidance, address your request to heaven in all sincerity from the depths of your being. Once you have made your request, stop thinking about it, and the answer will come. It may take a long time or it may come very soon. It may be brought to you by a bird, a sound, a phrase, another person or a dream. Of course, this requires that you be very attentive, but if you are, you will be amazed to see by what means the invisible world answers us.*

* Related reading: *The Wellsprings of Eternal Joy,* Izvor No. 242, Chap. 4.

15 January

*J*esus said, *'My Father and I are one.'* To be able to say such a thing, Jesus must have already done an immense amount of work. And, following his example, this is the work that we too have to do. Those for whom this identification becomes a reality live in a state of plenitude.

God is within us, just as his kingdom is within us. If you become conscious of being inseparable from the Creator, you will find that you see more and more clearly how to solve your problems, and above all, how to do good to those around you. Whereas if you are far off, you will be left to your own resources which are very limited. How sad that Christians reject the path that Jesus laid out for them! They should know that some Hindus are far more advanced in their understanding. When they practice Jnana yoga, the yoga of knowledge, they learn to meditate on the formula, 'I am He', repeating it within themselves until it becomes part of their flesh and blood. At that point, their own little, limited self no longer exists. It is the Lord and he alone who lives within them, and from then on they are capable of working miracles.*

* Related reading: *Man's Two Natures: Human and Divine,* Izvor No. 213, Chap. 3.

16 January

*H*uman beings can attain fulfilment only in a fraternal, collective life. Many people claim to be too busy to devote time to a collectivity, but for most of them, these occupations are in fact a form of psychological laziness; they prefer to live on the astral plane, or even lower, in the murky regions of the subconscious.

One day, when they find themselves bound hand and foot, these people will realize that they have been working for their worst enemies, those unknown creatures of darkness within them. It is these entities that have been ordering them about: 'I want to eat this... I don't want that... Go and get me that over there!' And they spend their time running about, pursuing pleasures and selfish passions to satisfy what they imagine to be themselves. It is time they understood that they have been nourishing the sworn enemies of their true happiness and must now make up their minds to participate in a fraternal life of generosity, love and light.

17 January

*T*he wealth of a spiritual person is extremely subtle, almost imperceptible, but if they become conscious of that wealth, heaven and earth are theirs. Why is it so difficult to understand this?

Someone will say, 'That is nothing new. I know that I cannot count on my material possessions, that they will not last. I know that they do not really belong to me and that I am going to have to give them up sooner or later, because I cannot take them with me to the next world. But even though I know all that, I still need to lead a materialistic life, it pleases me.' Yes, unfortunately this is often how it is: even when the intellect understands the advantages of one way, if the heart desires something else, what does the will do? It follows the desires of the heart; it does whatever pleases the heart. In order to live the rich, immense life of the spirit, you have to love it. It is not enough to understand it.

18 January

*M*aster Peter Deunov gave us this precept: 'Build your house on a foundation of kindness; let justice be its measure, love its delight, wisdom its limits, and truth its light.'

Kindness corresponds to the physical plane, justice to the etheric plane, love to the astral plane, wisdom to the mental plane, and truth to the causal plane.* In the hand, the thumb (which is linked to Venus) represents love; the index finger (linked to Jupiter) represents kindness; the middle finger (linked to Saturn) represents justice; the ring finger (linked to the Sun) represents truth; and the little finger (linked to Mercury) represents wisdom. When you work to cultivate these five virtues, you are working with the fingers of your divine hand, and this gives you great powers of action.**

* See note and diagram on pp. 396 and 397.

** Related reading: *New Light on the Gospels,* Izvor No. 217, Chap. 9.

19 January

Cosmic Intelligence has established certain laws that we must all know and obey. Many of you will think, 'But if we all have to conform to the same standards, we shall all be the same, like mass-produced objects.' No, you need not worry about that; you will continue to be different, because as you all have different temperaments, talents and qualities, you will not all be inclined to use the same methods.

Consider, for example, all the different types of yoga taught by the Indian spiritual masters: *Raja-yoga,* the yoga of mastery and self-dominance; *Karma-yoga,* the yoga of selflessness and altruistic activity; *Hatha-yoga,* the yoga of control of the physical body; *Kriya-yoga,* the yoga of light; *Laya-yoga,* which develops Kundalini energy; *Bhakti-yoga,* the yoga of love and fire, and so on. As disciples, we can all practise different yogas, but all yogas have the same goal: to teach us to rise to a higher plane and draw closer to the universal principle of truth.*

* Related reading: *'In Spirit and in Truth',* Izvor No. 235, Chap. 2.

20 January

Most people are proud of what they have managed to take, and they flaunt it for the whole world to see. But inwardly all their stolen wealth turns to dross. Yes, those who enrich themselves at the expense of others, whether individuals or countries, never really benefit from what they acquire. A time always comes when, even on the physical plane, they are obliged to give up their ill-gotten gains piece by piece.

The chief concern of truly spiritual people, on the other hand, is to give. When they greet you, look and smile at you, when they shake hands or talk to you, they constantly give you something good, something luminous. And in doing so, they themselves grow and blossom, and reach greater heights of perfection, because they are obeying the law of love, and the true law of love is to give.* But at the same time as they give, they also receive, for a stream of pure, transparent light flows to them from the sun.

* Related reading: *'In Spirit and in Truth'*, Izvor No. 235, Chap. 16.

21 January

There is only one way to be in full possession of our freedom, and that is to take the upward path. How can we do this? By trying to do the will of the Creator. Freedom does not exist in the absence of submission to God, to Him whom the Psalms call the Most High, and who is power, wisdom and love.

By distancing themselves from the Creator, whether consciously or unconsciously, people think that they are freeing themselves. In reality, they become enslaved by inferior entities who try to seduce and dominate them, just as the serpent seduced Adam and Eve and led to their expulsion from Paradise. For the serpent of *Genesis* symbolizes a whole category of malevolent beings who, having rebelled against God, want to drag human beings into their rebellion. This is why, in order to regain our lost freedom, we now have to join forces with the luminous entities that have always remained faithful to the Lord.*

* Related reading: *Truth, Fruit of Wisdom and Love,* Izvor No. 234, Chap. 18.

22 January

Rid your minds of the idea that you can transgress the divine laws with impunity.* It is easy to cheat human beings. They are so gullible and have so little judgement that anyone with a little guile can get them to do almost anything. Yes, it is unfortunate, but it is the truth. It is always possible to trick human beings, especially with lies, for they tend to prefer lies. If you tell them the truth, you can be sure that they will doubt what you say, but if you cheat and lie, you can almost always get what you want.

The only problem is, of course, that we are not here on earth in order to get our own way by conning other people. We must realize that one day we will have to answer for our actions before the great laws of the cosmos. Instead of amusing ourselves by putting on an act for the benefit of the blind, we should think about these laws. For all your actions are recorded, weighed and examined, and one day, you will have to settle your accounts. You may have gained a little something by deceiving the ignorant, you may have them under your thumb, but you yourself will have lost an entire kingdom in the world above.

* Related reading: *The Book of Revelation: a Commentary,* Izvor No. 230, Chap. 7.

23 January

Some people wonder how they will be able to recognize each other in the next world. It is love that enables people to recognize each other, for where there is love, there is knowledge.

How do dogs find their masters in a crowd? By their scent. Each being has a special scent depending on the quality of their love. The people you know as your friends today, in this incarnation, will leave you with a perfume that will remain within you for all eternity. It is also by the radiance of your love that you will be recognized in the invisible world. Every good deed, every sacrifice that you make for others remains with them as a perfume, and centuries from now, they will remember and recognize you.

If you love someone, you will be able to recognize them among the billions of beings in the invisible world – it is impossible to be mistaken. Amid the multitude of beings created, only your love for the person you are seeking will lead you to them. You do not even need to know their whereabouts on high.

24 January

Why do you think that happiness must necessarily come to you in the form you expect? There are so many different possibilities, but you cannot see them. You do not want to see them. You cling to your own ideas of happiness, hoping that one particular door will open for you... and it remains shut.

Instead of weeping in front of that closed door, why not think that there are perhaps others that are on the point of opening.* Suppose you expect great things of someone, and not only do they not give you what you had hoped for, but they are very unpleasant too. Well, rather than fixating on your disappointment, take a better look around, for there are sure to be others who are ready to help you. If you remain focused on your disenchantment and spend your time sending negative thoughts to those who have let you down, you will not see the friends gathering round you. It is in this sense also that your trials are useful: they oblige you to do or to discover things that you would never have done or discovered without them.

---

* Related reading: *The Seeds of Happiness,* Izvor No. 231, Chap. 5.

25 January

The principles of life and death manifest themselves both in human beings and throughout the universe. As soon as life shows signs of unfolding, opposing forces arise to subjugate and destroy it. Life must always defend itself. Knowing this, you must be vigilant and not allow negative forces to invade and overpower you. Of course, it is pleasant to let yourself go, but if you fail to react quickly, you will be paralyzed: the elements of your physical and psychic organism will no longer vibrate and put up a fight against these harmful forces, which will then take over your being.

Mud does not cling to a fast-spinning wheel because it is thrown off by the rapid motion, but as soon as the wheel slows down, mud builds up. It is up to you now to understand that you have much to gain by refusing to let yourself become flabby and lazy. Everything needs exercising: the physical body, the will, the heart, the mind, the soul and the spirit. If you respect this rule you will attain a level of vibration that throws off all impurities, and you will be able to advance for a very long time.*

* Related reading: *Life Force,* Complete Works Vol. 5, Chap. VIII.

26 January

*A*ttraction and repulsion are normal instinctive reactions. We like or dislike certain foods, drinks and activities. We like or dislike certain kinds of people. This is normal. We all come into the world with inclinations and tastes that tend to lead us in one direction or another. Yes, but if the Creator has also given us powers of reason and judgement, it is so that we may use them and not let ourselves be led blindly by our likes or dislikes. For our sympathies and antipathies, our attractions and repulsions are never reliable guides.

So, we must all study our likes and dislikes and see whether, by following them, we are helping or hindering our spiritual evolution. It is not a question of going against all our natural tendencies, for some of them are very good. It is a question of examining them, so as to give free rein to the good ones and redirect those that would lead us into difficult situations.*

* Related reading: *Golden Rules for Everyday Life,* Izvor No. 227, Chap. 70.

27 January

*T*he consciousness of human beings places them on the border between the lower and the higher worlds. If they are not vigilant, the forces of darkness drag them into their own realm where they grind them up and devour them. And once they have been devoured, they are spat out and there is nothing left of them. Whereas if they allow themselves to be drawn to and absorbed by the forces of the higher world, everything becomes clearer, and they become focal points of powerful, beneficial currents of light.

But although we must be careful to resist the lure of the lower world, we must not abandon ourselves wholly to the attraction of the higher world either. We must work with the forces of heaven, but without losing sight of the balance that needs to be maintained between heaven and earth. For our life is here on earth, and we must not leave it prematurely. Those who destroy this balance in order to reach heaven sooner may live in abundance and light, but they are not fulfilling their mission, which is to work on earth using the means of heaven.*

* Related reading: *Man's Psychic Life: Elements and Structures,* Izvor No. 222, Chap. 11.

28 January

*T*he work we do together through prayer and meditation has a beneficial effect on thousands of people throughout the world. It prepares their minds and hearts to desire and accept a new and luminous philosophy, a new, fraternal way of life. In this way, when they come across these ideas, they will not need any great explanations in order to understand them, because their psychic faculties, their sensitivity and intuition will already have been stirred and awakened.

The reason it is so difficult today for human beings to understand the spiritual life is that their spiritual sense organs, which should enable them to sense it and live it, are still asleep. In the new life, only a few words will suffice in order to feel and even to see all that is still invisible today. Then no one will be able to doubt the realities of the spiritual world.

29 January

*T*he vibrations of love are so powerful they can even influence stones. When you hold a stone in your hand and give it love, it will be impregnated with new vibrations. This is how Initiatic Science explains the power of talismans.* If an object is completely foreign to you and vibrates on a different wavelength, it cannot do you any good. But if you try to win it over and change its vibrations by giving it a great deal of light and love, you envelop it in the fluidic layers of your own emanations, and thereafter it will be your friend, capable of having a beneficial influence on your thoughts and feelings, as well as on your physical body.

* Related reading: *The Book of Divine Magic,* Izvor No. 226, Chap. 5.

30 January

We sometimes see drawings or paintings of a king seated on a throne, holding a staff or sceptre in his right hand and an orb or sphere in the left. The sceptre and orb represent the masculine and feminine principles.

The masculine principle is always symbolized by a straight line, a sceptre or caduceus, a pillar, tree, mountain or peak. The feminine principle is symbolized by a sphere, or by a round, hollow object such as a vase or chalice, or a chasm or cave. And the king who is holding the symbols of the two principles is not an earthly king; he is a spiritual king, an initiate who has a profound understanding of the science of the masculine and feminine, and who knows how to unite them within himself in order to create.*

* Related reading: *The Fruits of the Tree of Life – The Cabbalistic Tradition,* Complete Works Vol. 32, Chap. XXI.

31 January

*H*uman beings recognize that it is indispensable to have benchmarks and standards on the physical plane that no one can argue with. For years, for example, the Office of Weights and Measures in Sevres kept the standards that served as references for the whole world. Standards are always necessary, because if everyone decided as they pleased on the length of a metre or the weight of a kilogram, and so forth, it would be an indescribable mess. The appliances, machines and vehicles we use in our daily lives also need to be inspected from time to time – in some cases every day – to ensure that they are properly tuned.

Just as there is an Office of Weights and Measures in Sevres, there is also a cosmic centre by which we must set our standards. The sacred books say that God created the universe by measure, number and weight. The whole of creation came from this divine House of Weights and Measures, so this is where we must go to check our inner instruments: our mind, heart and will. It is vital that we adjust our instruments to the divine standards every day – and not just once, but three, five, ten times a day.*

* Related reading: *'In Spirit and in Truth'*, Izvor No. 235, Chap. 2.

1 February

It is thanks to women and their love of beauty that there is still some beauty in the faces and bodies of human beings, for it is they who transmit beauty to their children.

But women must learn to channel this need for beauty: instead of seeking it only on the physical plane, they should look for it also on the plane of the soul and the spirit. A woman who uses all kinds of artificial means to make herself pretty and charming for a few hours or even a day, may win the invitations she wants – she may even capture someone's heart. But if she does not try at the same time to acquire elements of eternal beauty, little by little her charms will fade. Whatever we do, our physical body wears out over time, and then it is the inner life that becomes apparent. So, our best solution is to work to acquire the inner beauty which, thanks to our luminous thoughts and generous feelings, will gradually be reflected by our physical body.*

* Related reading: *Creation: Artistic and Spiritual,* Izvor No. 223, Chap. 9.

2 February

*W*anting to be free without knowing what true freedom is or what to do in order to obtain it is the surest way to bind oneself and to suffer.

So many supposedly free people are, in fact, prey to entities of darkness! Yes, for every living creature requires nourishment, and evil entities prey upon any food they can get. If people who try to free themselves from all constraints are not intelligent enough to protect themselves, they are soon invaded by hostile entities. Then they scream in distress and cannot understand what has happened to them. Yet it is easy to understand: they were too foolish; they became like an inn with its windows and doors wide open to all the undesirable elements of the invisible world that ravage humanity. So many people who are considered unbalanced, insane or mentally ill are simply individuals who through ignorance exposed themselves to negative forces. They never thought that their mistaken notion of freedom would be the cause of such misfortune.*

* Related reading: *'Know Thyself'* – *Jnana Yoga (Part I),* Complete Works Vol. 17, Chap. X.

3 February

Human beings do not particularly enjoy hearing about loyalty and stability. Oh, how tedious, how difficult! Well, it is precisely this attitude that makes loyalty and stability even more tedious and difficult to achieve. You are the ones who make a particular quality easy or difficult to acquire. Why? Because if you dislike something, you will not attract it. You like change and dislike fidelity, so how can you expect to develop stability?

My analysis shows me that it is people themselves who repulse such or such a virtue – because they do not like it. In order to attract something, you have to love it! This is the magical aspect. Before trying to obtain something, try to love it, otherwise all your efforts will be in vain. It is essential to know this law.*

* Related reading: *Angels and other Mysteries of the Tree of Life,* Izvor No. 236, Chap. 15.

4 February

Look at a snowdrop: what strength, what power it has to be able to command the snow and the earth – 'Go on, make way, I want to come out!' And yet, it is so fragile, with petals so tender and delicate that a mere nothing can bruise them. But the earth and snow obey and give way to it. What is this power that compels the earth to open up? The snowdrop possesses incredible power in its tiny stem peeking through, and it triumphs. Love always triumphs.

And what about you? Are you not far stronger and more powerful than a snowdrop? You are, indeed, only you do not know how to go about it. Tell the difficult events, circumstances, obstacles and barriers: 'Come on, let me through, I want to get out! I want to free myself, to admire Creation and to pray. Clear the way!' And you continue, you persist the way a snowdrop does until the day you emerge and arise triumphant.*

* Related reading: *Love and Sexuality (Part II)*, Complete Works Vol. 15, Chap. IV.

5 February

We live in a world that has laws and customs that must be obeyed, and authorities that we must respect. This is well and good, but it is not enough. There are other, invisible authorities and laws that we must also take into consideration.

There is no point in winning the esteem of the whole world if we fail to win the approval of heaven. Human beings may applaud your achievements and give you prizes and grand titles, because they rely exclusively on appearances and external manifestations, but if heaven, which sees your inner thoughts, feelings and motivations, disapproves of you, you will never feel truly happy and content. Conversely, the whole world may be against you because it is incapable of appreciating what you do, but if heaven is with you because you have managed to win its approval, no amount of criticism or tribulation will destroy the happiness that dwells deep within you.

6 February

Suppose someone says, 'I realize that the spiritual life and Initiatic Science are beautiful, noble and grand. The trouble is that I was not given that light, and now I am in such a fix that I cannot seem to sort myself out.' Of course, that is quite understandable and excusable.

When you have never been instructed in this divine philosophy, it is entirely excusable to make mistakes. But once you know about this light, it is inexcusable to do nothing to improve your situation. How can you justify such an attitude before heaven? It is a serious matter. Once you have been introduced to the true philosophy that has guided all the noblest beings of humanity, you must do your utmost to study and apply it. The situation constantly improves for those who exert themselves.*

* Related reading: *Harmony and Health,* Izvor No. 225, Chap. 3.

7 February

Forget about some of those useless items of knowledge that so many people cram into their heads in order to show how erudite they are. In the new culture that is dawning, you will not be asked whether you have read such or such a treatise on the reproduction of insects, atomic fission, the religion of the Aztecs or of Cro-Magnon man. But you will be expected to cultivate love, selflessness, kindness, honesty and a strong will, for these are the powers with which humanity will have to work for all eternity. As for what you learn from books, if it does not help you to transform yourself and live in harmony, it will soon be forgotten.*

The world needs truly spiritual people, disciples who live a pure and luminous life in accordance with the divine laws, with the science of life.

* Related reading: *The Philosopher's Stone in the Gospels and in Alchemy,* Izvor No. 241, Chap. 14.

8 February

Do you imagine that a sage is always impassive and unmoved by feelings or emotions? Not at all! They can sometimes experience terrible inner storms, veritable tornadoes. But when this happens they know how to avoid being swept away: instead of submitting helplessly to the inner turmoil, they immediately concentrate and meditate so as to regain their inner peace. This is the difference between a sage and an ordinary human being.

This is why I keep insisting on the mental factor, for it is very important to understand that the faculty of thought must be given first place in your lives. At the first sign of inner distress or sorrow, summon your faculties of thought. Unfortunately, when it comes to agitating, troubling or gnawing at you, your thoughts are willing allies. But when you want to restore a state of inner peace and light, you do not seem to know how to involve your mental faculties. It is time you worked at this. Are you worried about something or in pain? Call on thought to help you, for when thought is present, it knows how to harmonize and remedy the situation.*

* Related reading: *The Powers of Thought,* Izvor No. 224, Chap. 8.

9 February

*O*ur organism has inexhaustible reserves. If there always comes a time when they seem to be depleted, it simply means that we no longer have access to them. Even when a person is dying and seems to have used up all their reserves, in fact no, they still have some left. It is just that they can no longer draw on them. If someone appeared who knew how to restore the contact and get the current flowing again, the patient would be saved.

That which alchemists called the elixir of everlasting life was not in itself capable of giving eternal life. What it gave was the power to purify, cleanse and clear obstructions from the conduits of the body so that those inexhaustible energies could flow freely. So, do not look for the elixir of everlasting life; work every day, rather, to purify and instil light into your thoughts, feelings, and actions, so that divine life may flow freely within you.*

* Related reading: *Sons and Daughters of God,* Izvor No. 240, Chap. 12.

10 February

Saturn is portrayed as an old man – or sometimes even a skeleton – holding a scythe. Saturn's scythe symbolizes time, which destroys all things, and the skeleton symbolizes eternity, that which withstands the ravages of time.

Saturn therefore represents both aspects. Behind the flesh – the world of appearances that time (the scythe) continually destroys – is the indestructible skeleton, eternity. A great deal of reflection and meditation is necessary before reaching the understanding that enables us to pass from time to eternity!*

* Related reading: *Angels and other Mysteries of the Tree of Life,* Izvor No. 236, Chap. 15.

11 February

Many legends can be interpreted as initiatic tales, and the objects mentioned in them symbolize the realities of the spiritual life. A knight, for instance, represents an initiate, and his shield or breastplate is a symbol for his aura. His sword is the light projected by means of his thought. The aura, which can be likened to a rampart that surrounds and protects us, represents the feminine principle; whereas thoughts that flash outwards into space represent the masculine principle. So, these two symbols – the sword and the shield – which date back to ancient times, represent the two principles: the passive principle, the aura, and the active principle, thought, which flies like an arrow – for an arrow, like a sword, represents the masculine principle.

In astrology, Sagittarius shooting his arrows is the symbol of the initiate who projects his thoughts to defend the city of light against the onslaught of darkness.*

* Related reading: *Man's Subtle Bodies and Centres,* Izvor No. 219, Chap. 2

12 February

The slightest event we experience in our lives is recorded within us. Psychologists call these records the memory or the subconscious. But whatever you call them, the important thing is to know how to use them. If you manage to live divinely – even if only for one second – eternity is in that second, and a recording exists which will live on forever. It is there, within you, and cannot be erased. So, whenever you feel ill disposed, uneasy or confused, open your inner record library and try to relive that moment of awareness in which you understood, however briefly, that your life could be one of light, peace, beauty, love and fulfilment…

Even if, for the time being, your situation and state of mind are vastly different from those moments of happiness, they are still there within you, and you can recapture them and feel their beneficial vibrations once again.

13 February

Several passages in the Gospels make it clear that Jesus respected certain aspects of the old order and the precepts received from Moses. But at the same time, he wanted to lead human beings further along the path of true religion.

For a spiritual master has exactly the same concerns as any other teacher: he must help his disciples to make spiritual progress just as educators try to help all their students to progress. He knows that many will be incapable of following his more advanced ideas and projects, but does this mean that he should neglect the few who are capable and who are eager to advance? Why should he set the bar at the level of the weakest and most limited? A master must keep urging human beings forward. Jesus did not destroy the religion of his forebears. He gave it greater depth and breadth, and internalized it. And if he returned today he would do the same with Christianity.*

* Related reading: *'In Spirit and in Truth'*, Izvor No. 235, Chap. 11.

14 February

*T*he moment you act, you inevitably trigger certain forces, which will just as inevitably produce certain effects. Originally, the word 'karma' referred primarily to this notion of cause and effect. It was only later that it came to mean the payment of a debt incurred through a misdeed.

In reality, one might say that 'karma' (in the latter sense) comes into play every time you do something less than perfectly – which is almost always the case! But human beings learn by trial and error. They have to practise before they can do things perfectly, and as long as they blunder and make mistakes, they have to keep correcting themselves and repairing their mistakes. And this, naturally, means pain and suffering.

You will say, 'Well, if whatever we do, we inevitably make mistakes, it would be better to do nothing.' There are people who have held this philosophy, but it is not a good solution, for if you do nothing you learn nothing. It is better to act, to make mistakes and to suffer, while trying, every day, to instil a little more kindness, purity and selflessness into your thoughts, words, feelings and acts. Gradually, you will no longer have to suffer any painful consequences, any karma. You will live increasingly in joy and fullness, and this is what is known as 'dharma'.

15 February

*T*he stream of water bubbling up from a spring carries away any twigs and leaves that threaten to block the flow. It is because it never stops flowing that a spring is always pure, always alive. Where can you find a better philosophy than that of a spring?

Model yourselves on a spring and become just like it, that is to say, love – never stop loving whatever happens. For this outpouring of love will protect you from impurity and suffering. You will not even notice when people try to soil or harm you, for everything bad will be carried away by the flow of water, of love. Day and night, hold within you this image of the spring that casts off evil and impurities. Never stop loving and you will suffer no more.*

* Related reading: *The Mysteries of Yesod,* Complete Works Vol. 7, Chap. III.

16 February

*T*hose who refuse to take into account the experiences of others show a misguided spirit of independence. Besides, whether they admit it or not, they cannot ignore them entirely.

What do novelists, poets and philosophers do? They live their lives then create works that generally reflect their own experience. Those works become a legacy and a source of nourishment for other human beings. So, we are constantly influenced by the experiences, both happy and unhappy, of others. Consciously or unconsciously, we absorb them, act upon them, and make them our own. This is why we should be thankful that there are books written by human beings who lived a higher life of wisdom, love, goodness and purity. It is fortunate that there are legacies from which we can truly benefit.*

* Related reading: *Alchemy, Astrology, Magic, Kabbalah – Aspects of esoteric science,* Complete Works Vol. 4, Chap. V.

17 February

Instead of allowing yourselves to be overcome by evil, endeavour to transform it. And, in order to transform it, you must try to learn the secret of unity. Take the earth as your model: the earth continually produces grass, flowers, trees, vegetables and fruit from waste, decaying vegetation and dead bodies. Yes, countless billions of corpses lie in the ground, and the earth, which rejects nothing, accepts them all. It is a veritable cemetery. But it is a cemetery that feeds all humanity. How is this possible? Well, it is because the earth knows the secret of transformation, which is the secret of unity.

The earth does not protest about all the filth that is thrown into it, or cry, 'What is all this? How dare you!' Nor does it try to reject or get rid of it. Instead, it starts up the special 'machines' that enable it to absorb, digest and transform it.* Yes, never forget this: the secret of true transformation is the secret of unity. Until you understand this, you will never resolve the problem of evil, because you will be working in the realm of duality.

* Related reading: *'In Spirit and in Truth'*, Izvor No. 235, Chap. 17, Part II.

18 February

Nobody has ever sufficiently emphasized the importance of being happy and contented. Most people do not realize how destructive a habit it is always to be dissatisfied with everything and everyone. What is even more serious is the growing tendency to consider contentment to be a sign of naivety and stupidity, whereas those who are constantly critical and discontented are considered intelligent.

A prolonged attitude of dissatisfaction, whether conscious or unconscious, is always corrosive. Dissatisfaction is acceptable only if it is directed at oneself. But no, people are dissatisfied with the Lord (He has not done things right), with life or with all humankind. Well, this harmful attitude will give you a lot of bad internal advice. So be on your guard: as we cannot prevent feelings from showing themselves, your face and gaze will become gradually sombre, your gestures brusque and your voice harsh. All this will make you very unattractive to others, for although people tend to think that the discontented are more intelligent, they find them very difficult to tolerate and keep well away from them.*

* Related reading: *Harmony and Health,* Izvor No. 225, Chap. 9.

19 February

In the new culture, human beings will learn to nourish themselves with light. You should not be surprised by this; it is within the natural order of things. All other forms of nourishment leave waste products that end by clogging and poisoning the system. Only light leaves no waste, for it is absolutely pure.

When you burn wood or coal in a stove, you have to clean out the cinders before lighting the fire next day. The same rule applies to our bodies. If you do not get rid of the wastes left in your body after eating and drinking, you will quickly fall ill or even die of poisoning. A great many illnesses are caused by waste that the body has been unable to eliminate. In fact, illness could be defined as the inability of an organism to get rid of certain wastes. Whereas, health is the result of a rapid and subtle exchange between the living organism and its environment, thanks to which all impurities are evacuated. Once you are able to assimilate light, that pure quintessence emanating from the sun, you will feel your health improving, your intelligence becoming enlightened, your heart expanding, and your will becoming stronger.*

* Related reading: *Harmony and Health,* Izvor No. 225, Chap. 7.

20 February

Human beings do not realize that their disorderly lives burn up their most precious quintessences. They think that these quintessences replenish themselves automatically. That is not so. It is true that certain materials can be replenished, for Cosmic Intelligence has designed the human body in such a way that it makes up for certain losses as it goes along. But if people refuse to act in accordance with the laws of wisdom, if they indulge in excesses of any kind, the losses are irreparable.

Those who live by the dictates of their instincts and passions without ever giving their soul or spirit a say, lose their most subtle quintessences. As they have no higher thoughts or altruistic feelings to counteract or improve their way of life, their energies are drawn exclusively from the physical plane, which is insufficient. In order to nourish their psychic and spiritual bodies, human beings need spiritual energies, and they can find these only by giving up certain inferior satisfactions – in other words, by making some sacrifices.

21 February

Many people have felt the influence of their thoughts and feelings on their physical body. But they usually notice this in the case of negative thoughts or emotions like hatred, anger, fear, anxiety or the distress caused by some bad news: the functions of certain glands are disturbed, and they feel as though they were being poisoned. So they know that negative emotions are bad for their health, but how many people make an effort to avoid such emotions in order to improve their psychic health? How many consciously decide to entertain only a positive, constructive state of mind?

It is surely easy to understand that if one can be poisoned by negative thoughts and feelings, one can equally be released, strengthened, vivified and resuscitated when one works with luminous, divine thoughts and feelings.*

* Related reading: *Hrani yoga – The Alchemical and Magical Meaning of Nutrition,* Complete Works Vol. 16, Chap. XII, Part II.

22 February

The four elements, which correspond to the four states of matter, are contained in the food we eat every day. So, by eating, we can connect with the angels of the four elements – the angels of earth, water, air and fire – and we can ask them to help us to build our physical body, and make it so strong, pure and luminous that it may become a fit dwelling place for the Christ, the living God.

By learning to relate to the angels of earth, water, air and fire, we receive particles of a subtler nature, and with these, we can build up our psychic bodies – even our body of glory. A human being who has succeeded in constructing this body of light (also known as the body of resurrection) becomes immortal.*

* Related reading: *The Yoga of Nutrition,* Izvor No. 204, Chap. 4.

23 February

*T*he Rosicrucian symbol is a red rose at the centre of a cross. The rose represents the heart, the fully developed heart chakra of a human being who, having attained their highest potential, is considered to be a sublimated cross. Humans make the heart chakra blossom through love, whose colour and scent are those of the rose.

So, the rosy cross symbolizes an initiate who, having worked to perfect himself, has brought the divine, pure, vivifying love of Christ to its full flowering within his own being. To be an adept of the rosy cross is to be versed in the secrets of all that pertains to the cross, as well as those that pertain to the rose blooming at its centre. The rose in the cross represents the perfect human being who not only possesses the knowledge of all the elements that constitute his physical, psychic and spiritual bodies and how they relate to the cosmos, but who also knows how to make the love of Christ spring forth and flow.*

* Related reading: *The Fruits of the Tree of Life – The Cabbalistic Tradition,* Complete Works Vol. 32, Chap. VI.

24 February

All the problems and dramas related to sexuality experienced by men and women stem from the fact that they have never learned how they should regard each other. If a man thinks of a woman as an object of pleasure, his behaviour will inevitably conform to that idea, and he will be obliged to follow the dictates of his passions. But if he sees her as someone to be loved and respected, someone who represents an aspect of the eternal feminine cosmic principle, the Divine Mother, he will be obliged to change his behaviour.

Jesus said, *'Let it be done to you according to your faith.'* Yes, things are what we make them by our attitude. This is a law of magic, which you need to understand and reflect upon. It is no good thinking that you can change the way you manifest your love without changing your attitude towards the object of that love. The manifestations will not change until your attitude has changed.*

* Related reading: *A New Earth – Methods, Exercises, Formulas, Prayers,* Complete Works Vol. 13, Chap. VII.

25 February

*F*ew people understand how important it is to keep themselves free for an enterprise, for work of a heavenly nature. They are always in a hurry to commit themselves, to become wedded to the world, and as the world is very heavy and terribly demanding, they are completely crushed under the weight of all that it imposes upon them. They have so much to do, so many duties to fulfil, that there is no longer any room in their head or their heart, no longer one minute in the day for their spiritual life.

Of course, they then use these obligations to justify themselves, without realizing that in doing so they are showing that they have been too ready to take on more than they can handle. If they want to save themselves, they must now snatch a moment, a space, out of each day and devote it to light, to the spirit.*

* Related reading: *On the Art of Teaching (Part III)*, Complete Works Vol. 29, Chap. III.

26 February

'*Let there be light!*' According to the account in the *Book of Genesis*, the creation of the world began when God uttered these words. Of course, the 'word' of God, which has nothing in common with what we think of as words, is but a way of expressing the idea that in creating, God projected something of himself. To say that God 'spoke' means that he willed to manifest himself. You find this very difficult to understand...

It might help to take an example from everyday life. When you have an idea, where is it located? Can we see it or find it in a particular part of your brain? No. We also have to admit that we do not even know what it is made of. However, as soon as you express that idea in words, its existence can already begin to be perceived. And when you finally act upon it, it is embodied in matter and becomes visible. Words, speech, are the intermediaries between the realm of pure thought and that of physical realization.*

* Related reading: *Angels and other Mysteries of the Tree of Life,* Izvor No. 236, Chap. 7.

27 February

Inhaling and exhaling, the ebb and flow of the two movements by which we alternately fill and empty our lungs: this is what keeps us alive. But breathing is a universal phenomenon. Everything in nature breathes – animals, plants, and even the earth itself.

Yes, since the earth is alive, it, too, needs to inhale and exhale. Of course, the rhythm of the earth's breathing is not eighteen breaths a minute like ours. It stretches over so many years that it is imperceptible to us. But it, too, dilates and contracts; its dimensions are never exactly the same. In fact, it is possible that earthquakes, tidal waves, volcanic eruptions, and such are due to this expansion and contraction. The earth is alive and it breathes; the stars, too, breathe. They breathe in, they breathe out, and their breathing is felt by us in the form of influences.*

* Related reading: *'Know Thyself' – Jnana Yoga (Part II),* Complete Works Vol. 18, Chap. XII.

28 February

The sages of India have given us a formula of very profound significance: 'I am He.' This is a way of saying, 'I have no existence as a separate, independent being. It is thanks to him, the Creator, that I exist; I am no more than a reflection. In seeking myself I will find He who created me. I am a non-being, an illusion. He alone is a reality.'*

God has disseminated his substance in billions upon billions of creatures. So, we may say that in reality, no creatures exist; only He, the Creator, exists, and we partake in his existence. In order to live this reality consciously, we have a tremendous inner work to accomplish.

* Related reading: *Man's Psychic Life: Elements and Structures,* Izvor No. 222, Chap. 13.

29 February

Most human beings consider that their ideal life would be to have a family, a job, a car and a house with all the modern amenities. This mediocre life is enough for them, and they are satisfied. From time to time, of course, they read a few books, listen to some music, go to see a show and travel. And that is all. They add nothing more powerful, more spiritual to their lives – they stagnate. They do not realize what dangers this slow-moving lifestyle poses for them: all kinds of physical and psychological illness are lurking there, just waiting for the right moment to infiltrate, bite and gnaw at them.

Cosmic Intelligence has not build human beings so wondrously just for them to slip into a sluggish and anesthetized state. It has prepared them to progress continuously along the path of evolution, supplying them daily with a current of life that sweeps away all physical and psychic mould and decay.*

* Related reading: *The Seeds of Happiness*, Izvor No. 231, Chap. 13.

1 March

*A*lthough they do not know it, human beings are immense. They know themselves in the divine world above; but they must get to know themselves here, too, through the medium of matter, and that is where the difficulty lies. Have you seen a cat playing with its tail? As the cat does not know that the tail is his, he chases it, bites it, and is astonished at the painful result.

You, too, are like a cat: one day, you discover the extremity of your being, here on the physical plane, and not realizing what it is, you give it a bite, and of course you scream because you discover that this trailing tail is a part of you. Our being is spread throughout space*, and one day we will have to get to know who we are. The 'cat's tail' represents our physical body, and now we must work to know ourselves through the matter of our own bodies. This is what makes our lives so difficult, but also so very worth living.

* Related reading: *'Know Thyself' – Jnana Yoga (Part I)*, Complete Works Vol. 17, Chap. VII.

2 March

*I*nstead of blaming everyone else for your difficulties, and even rebelling against God himself, reflect, meditate, and you will discover that these trials have a positive side. There are many qualities we cannot develop until we have passed through some suffering: setbacks, illness, and even the enmity of other human beings. Yes, that is why I will tell you that our enemies are often friends in disguise, because they force us to make the effort to progress.

Jesus said, *'Love your enemies'*, and many people find this commandment impossible, absurd even. How can we love people who have done us harm? The only way to love them is by discovering that they are friends in disguise, sent to us by Providence, to make us advance along the path of self-mastery and freedom.*

* Related reading: *Freedom, the Spirit Triumphant,* Izvor No. 211, Chap. 7.

3 March

*H*uman beings place too much trust in their intellect. They take it as a counsellor, even though it has misled them countless times! Yes, because the intellect sees only the appearance of things.

Listen to what a young girl's intellect says to her: 'Look at that boy. Not only does he have a good job, money, a fabulous car and expensive clothes, he is also charming, handsome, with the body of an athlete. You'd be a fool to pass up this opportunity – marry him!' That is the reasoning of the intellect, based on appearances alone. And once married, the young girl may discover that her charming athlete, who seemed so pleasing in every way, is cruel, selfish and dishonest. She could have avoided so much grief and suffering if she had asked the advice of her heart, her intuition, instead of listening to the workings of her intellect. Of course, this is just an example. Consider all the times in your life when your intellectual calculations have brought you only disappointment and regret, and draw your own conclusions.*

* Related reading: *The Symbolic Language of Geometrical Figures,* Izvor No. 218, Chap. 2.

4 March

We shall not genuinely transform society through revolutions, for they always result in the same disorder, dishonesty and injustice.* All that happens is that the torturers and their victims change sides, but they are still there. So, it is not outward changes that need to be made, but changes in people's mentalities.

Many people work to bring happiness to humanity, but how many of them know what human beings really need to be happy? Very few, which is why the results are not that great. And even if there is progress in some areas, we must admit that the situation is worse in others. True progress, true improvement first takes place in our thoughts, in our hearts and in our souls through our work with light. How can you expect changes to be effective if people's mindsets remain the same: self-centred, dishonest and deceitful? It is mentalities that need to be tackled – when mentalities change, the whole world will change.

* Related reading: *Love and Sexuality (Part II),* Complete Works Vol. 15, Chap. XXIX.

5 March

Symbolically, the legs and feet represent the physical plane. If you wish to be able to distance yourselves from the physical plane, work on your feet by means of thought. When you wash them, for example, get into the habit of touching them consciously, concentrating on the spiritual centres on top and underneath.

In Greek mythology, the god Hermes always appears with wings on his heels. Hermes symbolizes the Initiate who can travel through space, because he has discovered the secret of how to develop the spiritual centres in his feet. Until we know this secret, we cannot free ourselves from the physical plane, and we will not be allowed to leave our bodies to visit other worlds.*

* Related reading: *Spiritual Alchemy,* Complete Works Vol. 2, Chap. VII.

6 March

You wish to consecrate an object, and that is fine, but do you know how to go about it? In order to consecrate an object, you must begin by exorcizing it, for this object has already received the influences left by those who have touched it and by events around it, which have deposited fluidic layers on it that may be cloudy and impure. These layers form a barrier, a sort of screen, which prevents your thoughts from impregnating this object. Once it has been exorcized by prayers and even by burning incense, you can proceed to consecrate it, thus placing it under the influence of a heavenly power: it is then reserved.

It is as if a sign were placed on it. It is now impregnated with light: evil spirits can no longer lodge in it or make use of it, whereas heavenly entities can dwell in it, so that through it, they can help you with your spiritual work.*

* Related reading: *The Book of Divine Magic,* Izvor No. 226, Chap. 17.

7 March

*E*verywhere you turn you hear, 'Things must change. We need change.' And what are these changes? Always the same relentless struggles for power, money and honours, with some people pushing out others so they can take their place. No, there will be real change only when humans work to become more honest, more noble and more self-controlled – role models. But that does not interest people. What is the point of improving oneself? That is not what they need; they need positions to satisfy their selfish desires and cravings.

You may say, 'Yes, but if we follow your advice and try so hard to improve, to become good examples, the world is such that we will be left behind, ignored and unrecognized, on the bottom rung of the ladder.' On what basis do you jump to such conclusions? If you become a true wellspring, a sun, people will come to you and forcibly place you at the top to lead them, even against your wishes, even if you refuse. If that has not already happened, it is because you do not deserve it, because you are not yet ready.*

---

* Related reading: *Under the Dove, the Reign of Peace,* Izvor No. 208, Chap. 8.

8 March

There are people who are interested only in the occult sciences. They are proud to pass themselves off as astrologers, alchemists, magi and kabbalists, but the poor things do not realize that the appalling chaos of their lives has nothing to do with true astrology, alchemy, magic or Kabbalah. They would do much better to leave all these sciences alone!

It is in daily life that we must demonstrate that we know something. We manage to accumulate knowledge from books, of course, and may even become very learned; but this is not true knowledge. True knowledge is being able to master ourselves, to free ourselves from our weaknesses, and no longer be constantly prey to inner turmoil. True knowledge is the ability to be a benign presence that shines light all around.

9 March

Never deprive other living creatures of love. To love and be loved is the one divine right that the Creator has given them. Nobody has the right to prevent this. The question is to know how to love in order to avoid misunderstandings and suffering – but we must love. By seeking to perfect the way in which we love, we will succeed in drawing on the love that fills the universe.

Why do you think it is necessary to hold a man or woman in your arms in order to receive and give love? When we go for a walk with someone, when we talk with them, when we look at them and greet them, that is love, the most subtle, spiritual form of love. You have done this, haven't you? And you experienced a feeling of illumination. So, why not try to prolong this state, and even intensify it?*

* Related reading: *'Know Thyself' – Jnana Yoga (Part II)*, Complete Works Vol. 18, Chap. XI.

10 March

Childhood and maturity are two periods through which human beings are obliged to pass. We are a child for a time, and then we become an adult. That is true, not only in society, but also in our spiritual life. The only difference is that most people do not reach spiritual maturity at the accepted legal age of eighteen or twenty-one. Many people, even at ninety-nine, are not really adult, because they totally lack spiritual maturity.

Only those who have received the Holy Spirit can be considered true adults; the others are still just children. Yes, heaven looks on us as minors until we gain spiritual maturity, and we must maintain a childlike attitude, that is to say, always obedient, humble and submissive to the divine world. Every human being who is caught up in inextricable problems is still a recalcitrant child. True adults do not suffer, because they are always in the light.

11 March

People who take their difficulties or misfortunes too seriously find themselves in inextricable situations, for these problems can be overcome only when we begin to consider that they are not really that bad.

Believe me – your true Self is actually not affected by these tribulations. Your true Self is above all of life's vicissitudes. So, whatever the difficulties you may have to face, say to yourself, 'Of course, I can't deny that all these events are real, but is it really happening to me? No, because I am an eternal and immortal spirit, and what is going on here is happening to another person; it is just an illusion and I am a spectator.'*

* Related reading: *'Know Thyself' – Jnana Yoga (Part I)*, Complete Works Vol. 17, Chap. VIII.

12 March

Most people find the word 'magic' disturbing and are horrified if it is mentioned in their presence. And yet everyone practises magic; yes, on an unconscious level that is all they do. According to the laws of divine justice, every negative thought and bad feeling is in itself black magic, because it sullies and destroys. Conversely, all that brings harmony, all that is constructive, that brings beauty and enlightens, belongs to the category of white magic.

So, rather than protesting whenever magic is mentioned, human beings would do better to become conscious of the importance of how they behave. Yes, we see many people who have never opened a book about black magic, who do not even believe that such a thing exists, but those same people, because of the way they behave, think, feel and speak, are, in fact, veritable black magicians.*

* Related reading: *The Book of Divine Magic,* Izvor No. 226, Chap. 10.

13 March

If you cannot resist the inner impulses that torment you, it is because you have not developed enough love for the higher world of beauty, order and light. Your own willpower is not enough; we need the protection and help of heaven in order to resist. This protection, this help will come only if you really love perfection. As long as you do not have this love, you are sure to fall back into the traps of the astral plane.

So, if I see someone who boasts that they have conquered their temptations, but who does not love the sublime world, I can tell them, 'You will succumb, because you have no friend or associate to help you.' First of all, you must love the heavenly entities and invite them to be present within you. Then, because of these high and powerful allies, all your baser tendencies will begin to submit to their authority.*

* Related reading: *The Laughter of a Sage,* Izvor No. 243, Chap. 10.

14 March

Pride makes human beings poorer, and humility makes them richer. Yes, see how proud people behave – they are puffed up and full of themselves – whereas humble people empty themselves. It is precisely this emptiness that attracts plenitude, because as soon as there is a void, a force rushes in to fill it. One must be humble to attract God, for God cannot enter a vessel that is already full: you must be empty before He can enter.

If you say, 'God, I am foolish and You are wisdom, I am poor and You are wealth, I am weak and You are power', you are already creating space inside yourselves, and God will rush to fill that space. Whereas if you boast about your own virtues and abilities, you will never be visited by the Lord. He will say, 'Well, since you are so pleased with yourself, stay as you are – you do not need me.'*

* Related reading: *What is a Spiritual Master?*, Izvor No. 207, Chap. 4.

15 March

*D*uring your meditations, you must strive to focus your mental energy on a given point, a goal that you wish to attain. This goal can be personal, but it can also be collective. Ideally, it should be both personal and collective.

If you concentrate exclusively on the collective, forgetting yourself completely, you will exhaust yourself and you will soon have no more strength to continue your work. And if you concentrate exclusively on yourself, you will be at odds with the collectivity, forgetting that you are only a small part of a whole, with which you need sensible and harmonious exchanges if you are to maintain a balance, otherwise you will encounter obstacles and shocks. True wisdom teaches us to combine the two: to work for others, and at the same time, for ourselves.

16 March

You are ill and you take some medicine. It has curative properties, of course, but this will not suffice. It would even be ineffective if something within you did not also contribute to the healing process: the very substance of your physical body, which animated and exalted by your spirit, has the capacity to heal itself.

Medicine certainly fights illness, but at the same time, it weakens the body as a whole. What the body needs is to be given the chance to defend itself, and this is achieved by awakening the innate powers it possesses.

In the same way, a doctor should do more than prescribe drugs. A true doctor is endowed with a kind of magical power: their whole being emanates powerful fluids that penetrate the sick person, reviving them and restoring them to health. This is what should also be taught to medical students: that by their presence they can have a beneficial influence on their patients.

17 March

Inner peace is not something t
obtained directly without an interme̶d̶i̶a̶r̶y
the result of a synthesis of qualities and virtues.
It means that all the functions and activities
in a human being are perfectly balanced and
in harmony. Peace is a consequence of good
organization, of all the cells of all the organs
functioning perfectly. So no one will ever have
peace simply by saying, 'I want peace!'

Yet, observe human beings and you will see
that they all believe that peace would reign in
the world if they could only eliminate certain
things or certain people. Not at all! Even if
we were to rid ourselves of the army and all
its weapons, people would invent other ways
of destroying each other the very next day.
Peace is an inner state, it will never be obtained
by removing something external. It is within
ourselves that we must remove the causes of
war. And to live in a state of inner peace, we
must learn to bring our thoughts, feelings and
actions into harmony.*

* Related reading: *Under the Dove, the Reign of Peace,* Izvor
No. 208, Chap. 1.

18 March

*L*earn to love without waiting to be loved in return, and you will be free and able to do a great deal with this freedom. Unfortunately, human beings do not value freedom or try to obtain it; on the contrary, they do their best to tie themselves down. It is as if freedom weighs heavily on them, that it bores them and makes them feel at a loose end. Whereas, with constraints and even blows, at least they have something to do: yes, they can suffer, complain and weep. Well, that is not very bright.

Disciples must learn to resolve this question of love by understanding that what is most important is to love. Love all living creatures, day and night, like the sun that sends its love throughout space without bothering to wonder on whom that love might fall – on nobody or on the whole world – or whether or not some living creature might return that love. What is essential is that this energy, which comes from heaven, should flow through us, because this is what swells our hearts, filling us with wonder and inspiration.*

* Related reading: *The Splendour of Tiphareth – The Yoga of the Sun,* Complete Works Vol. 10, Chap. XIV.

19 March

Whether you are pure or impure is not revealed by a gesture or an action, but rather by the intention, the idea, the feeling or desire that lies behind that gesture or action. To be pure is to be able, in whatever you do, to rise within yourself and capture the most subtle, light-imbued elements. If your relationships with people are not inspired by this high ideal, even if you limit yourself to a few caresses and kisses on the pretext of remaining pure, you will still be acting out of impurity, and the effect will be the same as if you had indulged in debauchery.

Any contact or exchange that has a self-centred motive, and not a spiritual, divine aim, produces the same impurities. But if your sincere desire is to help, enlighten and sanctify the person you love, then that desire purifies both you and your loved one.

20 March

Every misdeed is an open door that allows evil entities to enter and torment you; so, the first thing these entities do, when they want to harm you, is try to entice you into doing something wrong. Suppose that you resist them and do not make any mistakes; then they are powerless. That is why I tell you that the devil possesses only the power that you yourself have given him. If you do not want to have anything to do with him, do not open the door to him. He does not force you; he just makes suggestions, and it is you who agrees.

Most people imagine that their troubles arrive suddenly, out of the blue. No, they prepare the conditions, throw open their doors and invite all these troubles in. How? By means of their inferior desires, thoughts and feelings, by means of certain weaknesses and misdeeds. At that precise moment, the devil sees an open door and goes inside.*

* Related reading: *Golden Rules for Everyday Life,* Izvor No. 227, Chap. 29.

21 March

*H*ow do you define true spirituality? When winter arrives, the earth receives less sunshine, and nothing grows. Even rivers freeze over. Life slows down. But in spring the earth receives longer hours of sunshine, everything grows and becomes beautiful, overflowing with abundant riches and burgeoning life everywhere. Well, spirituality can be compared to the action of the sun on the earth. When our spirit begins to radiate, penetrating all the cells of our body with its love and light, so that all our cells sing together in harmony – then, yes, we can claim to be spiritual.

True spirituality is like the radiance of the sun upon the earth: it is the spirit that vivifies and animates our body, so that light, peace and plenitude may dwell within us.

22 March

*E*very sacrifice we make for a sublime idea is transformed into gold, into light. That is the secret: the idea for which you work. If you work only for yourself, the effort you put into satisfying your own desires, needs, instincts, passions and greed is, in fact, energy lost.

The importance of the idea behind an action is not generally understood. Magic lies in an idea, a divine idea – the philosopher's stone that transforms everything into gold. That is why I say, 'Work so that light may triumph throughout the world, so that all people become increasingly aware of the bond that unites them as brothers and sisters, so that the kingdom of God may come on earth.' Everything you do to advance this idea is transformed into gold – into health, beauty, light and strength.*

* Related reading: *True Alchemy or the Quest for Perfection,* Izvor No. 221, Chap. 9.

23 March

*O*bserve how nature purifies water and you will notice that there are two possible processes. In the first, water filters into the ground, and there, in the darkness, it passes through different layers, leaving its impurities along the way. Little by little, it becomes limpid and clear and one day bursts forth somewhere as a spring. In the second, water is heated by the rays of the sun, becomes lighter and rises into the atmosphere as vapour, purifying itself through evaporation. Later it falls back to earth as dew or rain, bringing life to all vegetation.

Human beings, too, can purify themselves using two different methods. Those who do not wish to purify themselves by means of the sun's rays must descend into the earth and pass through dark regions – through difficulties, suffering and great stress. True disciples choose the other method: they expose themselves to the rays of the spiritual sun, rise and absorb the most luminous elements, and are thereby purified.*

* Related reading: *Life and Work in an Initiatic School – Training for the Divine,* Complete Works Vol. 30, Chap. VI.

24 March

We must learn that nutrition is not confined to the physical plane alone: it is a process that embraces the whole cosmos. Yes, because human beings have been created to make exchanges not only with the dense, but also with the subtle side of the universe, and we can find nourishment suited to each of our different bodies in the different regions of space.

Try to understand this, and you will begin to experience the universe as one immense symphony. But for these exchanges to be possible, the lines of communication must be kept clear. As long as they are not clear, nothing circulates freely. Like blocked pipes they must be unblocked. How? On the physical plane, we can change our eating habits, follow a diet, take laxatives, have enemas, and so on. On the psychic plane, we remove these obstructions by a rigorous screening of all our thoughts and feelings, retaining only the brightest and most generous ones.*

* Related reading: *Harmony and Health,* Izvor No. 225, Chap. 7.

25 March

*T*he Holy Trinity is placed on the central pillar of the Sephirotic Tree: the Father is in *Kether,* the Son in *Tiphareth,* and the Holy Spirit in *Yesod.* The Father is life, the Christ is light, and the Holy Spirit is love. Each sephirah corresponds to a part of the body, and *Yesod* is connected to the genital organs. The Holy Spirit has a great deal to do with love, and the saying that Jesus was 'conceived by the Holy Spirit' means that he was conceived in a state of perfect purity of consciousness.

It was Archangel Gabriel who came to announce this conception to Mary. Why? Because *Yesod* is presided over by the Archangel Gabriel.* Why was Gabriel chosen to bring this news to Mary and not another archangel? This becomes quite clear when we have studied the Kabbalah. The fact that it was Gabriel who came is very telling and is of great significance when we know the virtues and functions of each sephirah.**

* See plate and note on pp. 398 to 401.

** Related reading: *Love and Sexuality (Part I),* Complete Works Vol. 14, Chap. IX.

26 March

*A*ll day long people meet and exchange greetings, but they greet each other automatically, without thought or love. Even in families, even in couples. Look, the husband and wife kiss and hug – 'Goodbye, sweetheart! Goodbye, darling!' – but their gestures are empty. They act out of habit. In these circumstances, it is not worth bothering. We need to know how to give something vivifying and uplifting to the people we embrace.

Human beings still do not know how to embrace another, or when to do so. A man takes his wife in his arms to console himself when he is upset and unhappy, passing his sadness and discouragement on to her. Men and women constantly exchange with each other, but what is the nature of these exchanges? God only knows – or the devil, more likely! It is not forbidden to kiss someone, on the contrary; but you need to know how and when to do so in order to communicate eternal life to them.*

* Related reading: *Love and Sexuality (Part I),* Complete Works Vol. 14, Chap. XXII.

27 March

It is certainly true that human beings are often narrow-minded, nasty, ungrateful and so on, but why see only that one side? Of course, you must keep your eyes open if you are not to be misled, but that is only half of it.

If you are always suspicious and critical of those with whom you come into contact, they will not only stop manifesting their good qualities in your presence (and never forget that every living being also has a good side), but they will also seek revenge. Whereas if you show that you hold them in high regard and believe in them, you have a chance of getting through to at least some of them, and they will try to live up to your good opinion of them.*

* Related reading: *Man's Two Natures: Human and Divine,* Izvor No. 213, Chap. 10.

28 March

*D*uring the last supper with his disciples, Jesus took bread, blessed it, broke it and gave it to them saying, *'Take, eat, for this is my body.'* Then he took a cup of wine, blessed it, and gave it to them saying, *'Take this, drink it, for this is my blood. Do this in memory of me.'* The priest repeats these very same words and gestures at Mass when celebrating Communion. We cannot understand the true significance of Mass unless we realize that the Communion is the most meaningful part of a magic ceremony, in which bread and wine represent the two eternal principles – masculine and feminine – the foundation of all creation.

Then why is it that the faithful of the Catholic Church take communion only with bread – the host, Christ's body – representing the masculine principle? Wine – the blood of Christ – representing the feminine principle, is reserved solely for the priests. The faithful are therefore nourished with one principle only, the masculine principle: the feminine principle is missing. Yet true Communion requires the presence of both principles.*

* Related reading: *Cosmic Balance, the Secret of Polarity,* Izvor No. 237, Chap. 16.

29 March

Christians think of the cross as a symbol reminding them of the death of Jesus, but it has a far greater significance. It is true that it recalls the death of Jesus, but this is only one aspect. The crucifixion was an historical event, but the cross itself is a much vaster symbol – it is a cosmic reality – and we must understand it more broadly.

The most profound and complete meaning of the cross is the union of the two principles, masculine and feminine, and the work they carry out together throughout the universe. From the cross is derived another symbol: the hexagram, or Solomon's seal, made of two intertwined triangles. Here, triangles have taken the place of the straight lines of the cross, adding fresh meaning to its significance, but the idea is the same, and the same law applies – it is always about the work of the two principles.*

* Related reading: *The Mysteries of Fire and Water,* Izvor No. 232, Chap. 1.

30 March

*O*ur heart and intellect are useful, essential instruments, but they are not sufficient to guide us along all the paths we must travel. That is why we need to develop a third faculty: intuition. Similar to the intellect in that it is a kind of intelligence, and similar to the heart insofar as it is a form of feeling, intuition is both intelligence and feeling, but on higher planes.

'But that is clairvoyance!' you will say. No, people set great store by clairvoyance these days; there is a great deal of talk about it. But the faculty of clairvoyance allows you to see only the objective aspect (shapes, colours, movements) of the astral and mental planes.* You can be clairvoyant without understanding what you see, without knowing how to interpret it. So what good does that do you? Whereas with intuition, you may not have any visions, but you understand things much better than if you saw them, because you live and feel them.**

* See note and diagram on pp. 396 and 397.

** Related reading: *'Know Thyself' – Jnana Yoga (Part II)*, Complete Works Vol. 18, Chap. IV.

31 March

*T*he four cardinal feasts of Easter, Saint John, Michaelmas and Christmas take place at specific times throughout the year, and we must reflect on the universal events heralded by these feast days. Each of these celebrations corresponds to a season, an archangel, a planet, and a cardinal point.

Easter marks the beginning of spring; it is subject to the currents of Archangel Raphael, who represents the planet Mercury, and rules over the South. The feast of Saint John marks the beginning of summer, whose fires are supervised by Archangel Uriel, who represents Earth, and rules over the North. Michaelmas introduces autumn, under the influence of Archangel Michael, who represents the Sun, and rules over the East. Christmas marks the beginning of winter and is dedicated to the forces of Archangel Gabriel, who represents the Moon, and rules over the West. So, specific forces and entities set to work during each of these four major periods of the year, and we, too, at least through our awareness, should participate in this work.*

* Related reading: *Angels and other Mysteries of the Tree of Life,* Izvor No. 236, Chap. 12.

1 April

*F*or millions of years the sun has illuminated and warmed the earth, and it has done so without bothering who delights in these rays, or who contemplates them with gratitude, and who sleeps on underground. It is neither offended nor angry that people have not even realized they owe their lives to it. This is of no interest to the sun, and it continues to shine, giving them its blessings.

And like the sun, there are people who send their light and love through space, never bothering to know whether others benefit or not. They are happy, fulfilled, and find all their pleasure in distributing their riches throughout the universe. They have understood that the greatest happiness is to do what the sun feels and lives: to shine, enlighten, and warm.

2 April

It is not necessary to eat a huge amount in order to be in good health, but rather to assimilate your food well. And to assimilate food properly, you must chew it long enough to absorb all the elements it contains. Tell yourselves that the energy contained in a mouthful of bread is enough to send a train of a hundred carriages around the earth three times. So why does the train that you are go only a few yards with one mouthful? It is because you do not know how to extract all the energy contained in that one mouthful.

The same applies to the sun as it does to food. Try to learn to store up the sun's rays by means of your thoughts, for if you simply let them pass you by without doing anything, they will remain unused and ineffective. But if you consciously capture them and compress them within yourself, you open doors for them in your brain, and they pass through like fiery whirlwinds, nourishing your spiritual centres.*

* Related reading: *Harmony and Health,* Izvor No. 225, Chap. 5.

3 April

*T*he power of an atmosphere, an ambience, is enormous, because this is what brings out the good or bad side of people. That is why you must strive to be in an atmosphere of peace, harmony and light as often as possible. Of course, these effects do not often last beyond the time you spend in this ambience, but at least the lower nature is reduced to silence for several moments, and the higher nature can flourish. If you keep repeating this experience, one day the higher nature will finally become predominant.

Obviously, some people consider that toning down their lower nature is a sign of weakness; they feel much better giving vent to their domineering instincts and aggression – letting loose their wild beasts. But what damage these beasts wreak everywhere, devouring their children – in other words, their good thoughts and feelings, which are not yet firm and strong. We need to confine our wild beasts for a while, and that is what we seek to do by creating a harmonious atmosphere.*

* Related reading: *Golden Rules for Everyday Life,* Izvor No. 227, Chap. 81.

4 April

Most human beings are concerned solely with their own personal lives: looking after their daily needs, starting a family, and planning their leisure time. Of course, from time to time they contribute to society but, in general, their efforts are limited to their own affairs. However, whether they like it or not, they live in a collectivity, and if trouble were to break out in this collectivity, the safety of personal belongings and even lives could be at risk.

Focusing on our personal interests, possessions and families is not the best way to protect them, since there is always a danger that unforeseen disasters may sweep everything away. History is full of such examples. Be clear about this: selfishness has never proved a good solution for anyone. The only worthwhile solution is for each of us to think how best we can help to improve the collectivity. If we do this, then everyone will be safe.*

* Related reading: *A Philosophy of Universality,* Izvor No. 206, Chaps. 7, 8 and 10.

5 April

The way must be open so that life may flow, light may shine through, and celestial currents may enter: this is an immutable law of nature. Why are gemstones so valuable? Because they let the light shine through them. If nature has managed to work with astonishing success on certain materials, refining, purifying and colouring them to produce the marvels we admire today – crystals, diamonds, sapphires, emeralds, topaz, rubies, and so on – why shouldn't human beings accomplish the same work on themselves?

What are prayer and meditation? They are the very activities that enable us to purify and illuminate everything within us, until one day, we become as transparent as gemstones, and the Lord, who appreciates precious stones, will then place us in his crown. This is symbolic, of course, but it is absolutely true.*

* Related reading: *Looking into the Invisible,* Izvor No. 228, Chap. 7.

6 April

It is said in the *Zohar*: 'We have learned that the Book of Concealment is the book of the equilibrium of balance.' But this equilibrium does not mean there is no movement. When God polarized Himself for the purpose of creation, the scales began to move, to sway upwards and downwards. The act of creation presupposes the perpetual motion of the two pans of the scales, and this alternation will continue until such time as the work of creation is complete. This movement of the scales tells us that creation is still a work in progress.

Perfect equilibrium prevents any exchange, yet life consists entirely of exchanges. However, this movement must be measured, for if one side of the scales rises too high, the other falls too low, and then it collapses: all oscillation stops, and so does all life. What we call balance is, in reality, an imbalance; equilibrium momentarily upset, and then immediately restored. This change in the level of the scales releases forces, which must be rapidly balanced by a movement of contrary forces to be kept in check. It is this fluctuation that generates life, and we can conclude that life is an imbalance continuously being rebalanced.*

* Related reading: *Cosmic Balance, the Secret of Polarity*, Izvor No. 237, Chap. 2.

7 April

Whoever you are, and wherever you may be, you will encounter adversaries with whom you must struggle. But there are two kinds of struggles: either you do away with your enemies or you spare them. If you do away with your enemy you will no longer have to struggle, and that will be a disaster, as you will no longer make progress. If you spare them so that you can contend with them for the rest of your life, you will become strong.

Very many people try to rid themselves of their enemies, and what happens when they finally succeed? They are not any happier; they feel that something is missing for they needed to pit themselves against their enemies. So instead of destroying your foes, learn how to go about becoming better and stronger, and you will help your enemies to improve at the same time! But you will succeed only if you consider them as indispensable agents for your evolution.*

* Related reading: *Cosmic Balance, the Secret of Polarity,* Izvor No. 237, Chap. 7.

8 April

Many people claim to be inspired by heaven. They gesticulate, roll their eyes around and ramble incoherently, or spend hours frozen in some posture of simulated ecstasy. Well, in reality, these people are unbalanced and sick, and the rest of their behaviour proves it. They may talk about heaven, the Holy Spirit, angels and archangels but, in fact, they are ill. They believe they are communicating with the divine world, whereas lack of discipline and inner work has connected them with the subterranean regions of the astral plane.* They receive messages and commands, indeed, but of a kind they would do well to mistrust.

We must learn to distinguish between inspiration and various forms of mystical delirium. Those who are truly in contact with heaven can receive only waves of light, harmony and peace.**

* See note and diagram on pp. 396 and 397.

** Related reading: *Looking into the Invisible,* Izvor No. 228, Chap. 18.

9 April

We owe everything to nature: all the elements that form our bodies, all that sustains us – water, food, air to breathe, the light and heat of the sun – all the materials for our clothes, houses, tools, and so on – everything. Human beings take great pride in their ingenuity, but where do they get all the materials used to make their instruments, appliances, and even their works of art? From nature.

Nature provides us with everything. But the details of what we take are noted somewhere. We have incurred these debts with nature, and we must settle them. How can we do so? With a payment called respect, gratitude, love, and the willingness to study everything written in the great book of nature. Paying means to give something in exchange, and we can do this with all that is good in our hearts, our intelligence, our souls and spirits. We are limited on the physical plane, and nature does not insist that we return all the food, water or air we have taken. But on the spiritual plane our possibilities are infinite, and it is on that level that we can repay a hundredfold all that nature has given us.*

* Related reading: *A New Earth – Methods, Exercises, Formulas, Prayers,* Complete Works Vol. 13, Chap. VIII.

10 April

When you care for a child by thinking about its soul and spirit, you attract the blessings of its guardian angel. Every small child has an angel at its side to look after it, wanting to uplift it, but so often, this task is met with great difficulty because the child is exposed to harmful, evil influences.

The guardian angel is constantly present, keeping a close watch over the child, but can do very little on the physical plane, and that is why it is so very happy to see someone – a father, mother or teacher – showing the child the way of goodness and light. The child's angel rewards such people with gifts of light and joy.

11 April

The true tragedy of human beings is that they expect to receive what people are incapable of giving. Then, when they are given something precious, they neglect it, because they were expecting something else.

Just look around: do human beings show gratitude to their Creator? No, they even blame Him for all kinds of reasons. Are children really grateful to their parents? So often these parents are made fun of and criticized. And the grievances that disciples harbour towards their Master do not bear mentioning! He may give them every conceivable method to help them work toward personal perfection, to become children of God – luminous and radiant – no, no, that is not what they want. They want success, power and glory, and they blame their Master for not granting their desires. Dear Lord, what can be done with such people? It is not surprising they are forever unhappy. Let them learn to give a little in return for everything they have received from God, from their parents, from their Master – if they have one. Let them at least find some feeling of gratitude, and they will then find peace and joy.*

* Related reading: *Cosmic Balance, the Secret of Polarity,* Izvor No. 237, Chap. 12.

12 April

Human beings court misfortune because they do not see the dangers awaiting them if they make such and such a decision, or launch into such and such a venture. They set out so happily, without insight or foresight, and throw themselves head first into difficulties. If only they had known how to develop their inner vision, they would have been warned, because that inner sight, known as the third eye, is like radar, sending out waves that return with warning of obstacles along the way. But in most people this radar has broken down because the disorderly lives they lead prevents it from working properly.

It is true that there are cases when this spiritual eye, however well developed, does not give us due warning: when the Twenty-Four Elders, the Lords of Destiny, have decreed beforehand that certain events must necessarily come to pass. Even though we may sense or see them coming, we cannot avoid them, and must cope with them with the light of Initiatic Science. But generally, if we have prepared the right conditions for it, this spiritual eye is there to warn us and guide us.*

* Related reading: *Looking into the Invisible,* Izvor No. 228, Chap. 10.

13 April

*O*ver the centuries, for most people, religion has been reduced to a set of practices in which their inner being does not take part. Clearly, these practices were unable to awaken and develop the spiritual centres within them; they have even ended by covering these centres under impenetrable layers. So now, these people pray and meditate in vain, seeing and feeling nothing – neither angels, nor archangels, nor nature spirits – nothing. They do not even suspect that hostile entities, wanting to harm them, may be present.

Sheep feel the presence of a wolf prowling around their flock, and are visibly afraid; the shepherds notice and take precautions, knowing that the wolf is lurking nearby. How is it that sheep sense the presence of a wolf, whereas human beings have no idea that evil entities are prowling around, intent on causing harm?*

* Related reading: *The Faith that Moves Mountains,* Izvor No. 238, Chap. 4.

14 April

Many jobs are difficult, but leading human beings along the way of light and divine love is the most difficult of all. This requires the preparation of many incarnations; one must even be created specifically for such a calling.

Yet so many people imagine they are capable of guiding others! They 'set up shop' to attract disciples, to whom they deliver fine speeches but, unfortunately, that is not enough. For it never occurs to them to correct all their own many deficiencies and imperfections, and these are clearly reflected in the advice, teaching and guidance they give. This is why instead of getting their disciples to climb up the steep tracks toward the sublime heights, they direct them along wandering paths scattered with pitfalls. Indeed, they themselves are often dragged over a precipice.*

* Related reading: *What is a Spiritual Master?* Izvor No. 207.

15 April

*O*ur physical body is built symmetrically on either side of a central axis – the spinal column – and in this regard, it can be said to be governed by the number 2. We have 2 eyes and 2 ears, and although the brain and nose seem to be 1, they are really 2, with 2 hemispheres and 2 nostrils. Then there are 2 lungs, 2 kidneys, and, lower down, a man has 2 testicles and a woman 2 ovaries. Finally, we have 2 arms and 2 legs.

Even though this symmetry is rarely perfect, as the left side of our bodies is never an exact replica of the right, still it remains a physical fact. But our psyche is quite different. Studies of the human brain show that the functions of the two hemispheres are not identical: the left hemisphere controls all analytical faculties (logic and reason), which can be described as masculine, and the right hemisphere is the seat of the faculties of synthesis (intuition and sensitivity), which can be considered feminine. So the activities of these two hemispheres are complementary. We can therefore say that our physical bodies are constructed symmetrically, whereas our psyche is based on the polarization of masculine and feminine – positive and negative.*

* Related reading: *Cosmic Balance, the Secret of Polarity,* Izvor No. 237, Chap. 9.

16 April

*T*o master our feelings and thoughts, we must begin by watching over our every little gesture in daily life. In this way, we will gradually acquire the psychic control that will then allow us to master more powerful forces. You might say that you do not see the connection. Well, that is exactly the issue: as long as you have not learned to control the smallest details about yourself, you can never hope to control anger, contempt, envy, disgust, the desire for vengeance, and so on.

If you were to pay attention to the way you speak, you would soon notice that you are not even able to control your hands – you wave them around, scratch yourself, fiddle with the buttons on your clothes, and so forth. So, begin by learning to keep your hands still. How can you hope to master the powers that are beyond you, if you cannot yet control your tiniest instinctive movements?*

* Related reading: *The Path of Silence,* Izvor No. 229, Chap. 4.

17 April

*T*ake the physical world, the spiritual world and the divine world – or, if you like, the form, the content and the meaning – or again, the world of action, the world of laws, and the world of principles: yes, it is always the same trinity – the body, the soul and the spirit. The spirit is an expression of the divine world, the soul corresponds to the spiritual world, and the body corresponds to the physical world. So the soul lies between matter and spirit: it is an intermediary, a vehicle that transports elements from heaven towards the earth, and from earth toward heaven. Everything that travels downwards or upwards passes through the soul. The spirit can only reach downwards, and the body can only reach upwards, but the soul moves up and down between the two. This is why the spirit has power over matter only by passing through the soul.

Observe what happens in nature: the sun cannot act directly on the earth; it needs the intermediary of air and water. In the same way, our spirit cannot touch our physical body directly; it can only act through a go-between – our soul.

18 April

*D*oes God exist, or not? The answer is really very simple. To the non-believer, it is true that God does not exist. For whether things exist or not depends on us. Take a man who is asleep: even if all the world's treasures are heaped around him, as he is completely unconscious, he cannot delight in them. Almost all human beings are plunged in a similar state of profound unconsciousness.* Only the Initiates, who are truly awake, see the splendours surrounding them, and marvel. Everyone else has these same riches both within and around them, but they remain unconscious of this wealth.

So it all depends on our state of awareness. When we are awake, some things take on reality, and when we sleep, they fade away. It is the same with God: if we are asleep we do not sense His presence, so we claim that He does not exist. But as soon as we awaken, we feel God living inside us and all around us.

* Related reading: *The Faith that Moves Mountains,* Izvor No. 238, Chap. 9.

19 April

*J*esus said, *'Do not throw your pearls before swine'*, because it is unwise to reveal spiritual truths to those who are not prepared to receive them.* But for those who are ready, knowledge of these truths is most desirable, for Jesus also said, *'Know the truth, and the truth will make you free.'*

What is more important than being free? And it is precisely truth that has the ability to liberate. Truth liberates, just as love warms, and wisdom enlightens. Each quality and each virtue has its own particular properties, and that of truth is to set free, because truth is linked with the will, with strength.

* Related reading: *What is a Spiritual Master?*, Izvor No. 207, Chap. 3.

20 April

*S*pace is inhabited by billions of evil entities who have sworn to ruin humankind. Of course, it is also populated by billions of luminous entities who work to help and protect us. Yes, but their aid and protection will never be truly effective if we do nothing to progress along the right path.

Nor is any Master able to protect us if we insist on living in an unreasonable way. A Master instructs us, enlightens us, and will even try to influence us through his thoughts and feelings; but if we destroy all his good work by opening our doors to dark entities through carelessness, frivolity and lack of good will, what more can he do?*

* Related reading: *Golden Rules for Everyday Life,* Izvor No. 227, Chap. 112.

21 April

*M*any scientists believe they can justify the deadliest discoveries by the simple claim that they are working for the good of their country, and therefore fulfilling the highest moral duty. Well, as far as Initiatic Science is concerned, this claim is invalid, because Initiatic Science is a universal science that takes no account of borders, and stands far above all forms of limitation. This science teaches what is truly good or bad, moral or immoral for the whole world. So, if we turn to this science for an opinion, it will state unequivocally that behaviour that is good for one country and bad for all others can never be justified.

To Cosmic Intelligence, the most important thing is always the goal we work towards, and how we use the energy and talents that we have been given. So, only people who make use of every one of their inner gifts in the service of the kingdom of God are always, whatever they may do, approved, accepted and glorified on high.

22 April

*H*uman beings left the womb of the Eternal to undertake a long descent into matter, so they need everything that matter has placed at their disposal in order to survive. Now that we have become so far separated from the Source, it is impossible to return there easily and directly without any support, without material tools or instruments; so it is only wise and reasonable to make full use of the material means we do have. Only, we should not use these aids to dissipate our energies and distance ourselves even further from the Lord, but rather to return toward unity.

So it is our goal that counts, the direction we take as we make use of everything the material world has provided. Whether we are eating, breathing, walking, working or loving, it is all fine as long as we mobilize everything toward our return to the divine Source.*

* Related reading: *The Path of Silence,* Izvor No. 229, Chap. 11.

23 April

We can never really make valid judgments on good or evil, because nothing is ever either wholly good, or wholly bad. Even the best things in life have their drawbacks. Just think of the arrival of spring. On the one hand, it is wonderful – light and warmth make everything bloom. Yes, but bugs flourish too – wasps, flies, caterpillars, aphids and mosquitoes abound. And what of technical progress, is it good or bad? Many discoveries that initially brought immense improvements ended up producing catastrophes, because human beings failed to be prudent and foresighted enough to reflect on the possible consequences. There is no need for me to give you examples, you can see for yourself every day.

So, whatever the conditions or events, precautions must be taken. The very best things can turn out badly for those who are ignorant because they are not prepared to deal with them. Whereas, for those who are wise and know how to work, it is the opposite – they make progress amid the most difficult trials.*

* Related reading: *Cosmic Balance, the Secret of Polarity*, Izvor No. 237, Chap. 7.

24 April

*T*o be simple is to know how to unify our thoughts and desires. As long as you allow free rein to all sorts of contradictory thoughts and desires, your lives will be complicated and disorderly, and you will complain, 'I feel lost!' Those who complain that they are lost show that they have desired and accumulated an ill-assorted collection of things, plunging them up to their necks in complications.

The reason why diamonds are so precious is that they are unalloyed, pure carbon. Add another element, and it is no longer a diamond. It is the same with disciples: if they wish to taste, touch, know and experiment with everything, they will lose their value – they will no longer be diamonds, just opaque stones. True disciples must aim for a single goal, have one ideal, one desire, and only one food, symbolically speaking. If they do this, they will live in the simplicity of light.*

* Related reading: *Golden Rules for Everyday Life*, Izvor No. 227, Chap. 27.

25 April

*E*very being needs to think in order to satisfy the intellect, to feel emotion to satisfy the heart, and, finally, to act so as to satisfy the will.

But it is through action that we know the greatest joy. Fulfilment is not found in understanding or feeling, but in achievement. When we perform an action, we feel in tune, at one with the primordial force. Action is the result of the concentration of all our energies, with the participation of every cell in our being, leading to its successful achievement.* This is why every act of kindness, wisdom, selflessness and love carried out with full awareness brings us fulfilment.

* Related reading: *The Living Book of Nature,* Izvor No. 216, Chap. 5.

26 April

The masculine principle is the emissive principle, which projects and inseminates, providing the seed of life. And the feminine principle is the principle that gathers and organizes to produce a finished, perfect piece. So the work of creation is shared between the two principles, and we must never overestimate or underestimate the importance of either one. The question is not whether one principle is more important or necessary than the other: both are equally important, equally indispensable, but in two different realms.

The masculine principle sends out waves or lines of force, which would be of no use if the other principle were not there to respond, to receive and to work on all it has received. It is these two principles that make life possible: they work together out of sight, even inside the physical body. It is only when one becomes too dominant to the detriment of the other that anomalies and imbalance appear. The science of the two principles is the science of cosmic balance.*

* Related reading: *The Symbolic Language of Geometrical Figures,* Izvor No. 218, Chap. 3.

27 April

Thought must always come first and must preside over everything; the rest – feelings and desires – must take second place. Suppose you put feeling first and thought afterwards: you will give in to your impulses and inclinations, without reasoning or reflecting. Well, this would lessen the value of your activities and might even land you in trouble.

This does not mean that you should suppress all feeling – no, you would be depriving yourself of the immense wealth contained in matter, which needs to be elaborated by thought. What is important is to put thought in first place, and then you will always find the best solutions, and the best course of action.*

* Related reading: *The Powers of Thought,* Izvor No. 224.

28 April

Do not imagine that a Master, who has dedicated his life to helping human beings, does not see their negative side. He sees it, and is especially skilled in detecting it, but he does not dwell on this aspect because he knows that we cannot help people by stressing only their faults and failings. In fact, this attitude could even make them worse. A sage knows that men and women are all children of God, and he approaches every being with this thought foremost in mind. In this way, he works as a creator, developing the divine side in everybody he meets, which makes him happy too.

This is the best way to deal with people: try to discover their qualities, virtues and all their inner riches, focus on these, and you will help them develop their gifts.*

* Related reading: *What is a Spiritual Master?*, Izvor No. 207.

29 April

Some people consult clairvoyants to know what their future holds.* Well, I should tell you that we do not need clairvoyants for that, because it is very easy to know our future. Of course, we may not be able to guess what our future professions, encounters, financial gains or losses, illnesses, accidents, or successes will be, but none of that is very important.

What is essential is to know whether or not we will advance along the path of evolution, and if we will find freedom, light and peace – and this is easy to discover. If you love all that is great, noble, just and beautiful, and if you work with all your heart, mind and will to realize this objective, your future is already mapped out for you: one day, you will live in conditions that correspond to your ideal and aspirations. There! That is what you need to know about your future. The rest is of secondary importance, because it is transient: it may be granted you, and then taken away again. When you leave the earth, only the aspirations of your soul and spirit will truly remain with you.

* Related reading: *Looking into the Invisible,* Izvor No. 228, Chap. 5.

30 April

*T*he whole of space, from the e
sun and far beyond, is inhabited by be...
four elements – earth, water, air and fire – are
inhabited by creatures mentioned in all traditions
of the world. Of course, they may not be exactly
as each religion or culture describes them, but
these beings do exist, and we can communicate
with them and persuade them to participate in
our work for the coming of the kingdom of God
on earth.

When you walk in nature, try to be conscious
of the presence of all the spirits around you,
and realize that they already lived here long
before human beings appeared on earth. Link
yourselves with them, speak to them and marvel
at the accomplishment and beauty of their work
in lakes, rivers, forests, mountains, clouds, and
so forth. This will make them happy, and they
will befriend you and give you gifts of vitality,
joy and inspiration.

1 May

*T*he sun sends out light and life which the earth, human beings, animals and plants receive. We absorb this life and, on both the physical and psychic planes, we then discard waste which the sun transforms and purifies and returns to us in the form of new life. This constant exchange between earth and heaven also exists between ordinary human beings and the Initiates. The Initiates gather the raw material of ordinary human beings, transmute it, and give it back to them in the form of spiritual treasures.

If we are serious in our desire to evolve, we must not complain about the faults and failings we see in others. Instead, we must work to transform these failings within ourselves so that we can give them back in the form of light. By working to transform the vices and weaknesses of those around us, we are working for the kingdom of God and, one day, the Initiates will accept us as disciples. They will tell us, 'Come and join us, for we need more workers, and you are capable of helping us.'*

* Related reading: *Spiritual Alchemy,* Complete Works Vol. 2, Chap. IX.

2 May

People sometimes tell me, 'The more I think, the more I reflect, the unhappier I become. So that's it, I'm not going to rack my brains any more, I will simply let things take their course.' Well, this is a recipe for failure.

The capacity to think, to reason and reflect, is the best gift God has given us. Why would we want to do away with it? It would be just like walking blindfold along the edge of a cliff. Of course, to think and understand often causes us to suffer, but it is the only way to evolve. In reality, there are two kinds of thought: one that brings grief and suffering (because we have not learned how to think or what to think about) and one that brings peace and joy. Analyze yourselves and you will see that this is so. Therefore, try to entertain only thoughts that will help you to stand tall.*

* Related reading: *Freedom, the Spirit Triumphant,* Izvor No. 211, Chap. 1.

3 May

*T*he one true religion is the solar religion. This does not mean that other religions are false or bad. No, but they are true only to the extent to which they coincide with the solar religion. How many religions are there in the world about which we know practically nothing! And how many more have disappeared or are destined to disappear! Even the Christian religion may disappear but, if it takes its inspiration from the solar religion, it will be born again in another form, for – although Christians have never understood this – the religion brought by Jesus was a solar religion. For example, when Jesus said, *'Be perfect, as your heavenly Father is perfect,'* how could we have any notion of perfection if we do not take the sun as our model?

If you want to become truly perfect, the only possible being that can serve as a model is the sun. Not the saints, not even the Initiates. The saints and Initiates can certainly give us an example of great virtue, but they know that they are as nothing compared with the sun. This is why their bearing is always humble; they bow before the sun. They know that whatever they do, their light, warmth and life can never compare with the light, warmth and life of the sun.

4 May

Each one of us comes to earth with our particular tastes and tendencies and, however hard we try, there is nothing we can do to change them. This is why it is so important to recognize the true nature of the people you associate with, so that you do not expect them to manifest something that is not in them. They may make an effort in order to please you, but it will not last, for we cannot ask people to go against their true nature.

Try telling a cat that it must not eat mice: it will say 'meow' in agreement – but as soon as it hears a faint scratching sound, even if you are still preaching to it, it will be off in a flash to catch that mouse without the slightest remorse. The mouse interests it far more than your sermon. This is its nature. So, do not have too many illusions about the effect your words will have next time you tell a cat not to eat mice – symbolically speaking.*

* Related reading: *Love and Sexuality (Part II)*, Complete Works Vol. 15, Chap. XVIII.

5 May

*M*editate on the image of a tree. A tree consists of roots, a trunk and branches, and the branches bear leaves, flowers and fruit. The roots of a tree live deep underground in total darkness, where they work to absorb nutrients from the soil and to produce the raw sap, which then rises through the trunk. Far from air and light, roots carry out an arduous, thankless task fraught with obstacles, difficulties and constraints.

The trunk, on the other hand, rises heavenwards, bearing currents of intense life: at the core are the upward channels carrying the raw sap, while the elaborated sap flows down through channels lying along the outer edge of the trunk. As the trunk grows taller and stronger, it acquires new branches that sway joyfully in the wind and light, and display the life and beauty of their leaves, flowers and fruit for all to see. What a contrast between the upper and lower parts of a tree!*

* Related reading: *Truth, Fruit of Wisdom and Love,* Izvor No. 234, Chap. 18.

6 May

In certain circumstances instinct can be a reliable guide, but in others it would be better not to follow it. When human beings were still at a very primitive stage closer to animals, instinct was their best guide. But once the development of the brain had raised them to a higher level, they began to have other guides – reason and intelligence – which they must follow. So, what was good in the past is no longer fitting today.

Take fear, for example: fear is a useful, in fact, indispensable guide for animals, which keeps them safe and teaches them how to avoid danger. But fear is no longer permitted to human beings. This is why the goal of initiation has always been to teach disciples to conquer fear. Fear and death are the two great enemies that have to be vanquished, and they are vanquished by love and knowledge.*

* Related reading: *True Alchemy or the Quest for Perfection,* Izvor No. 221, Chap. 5.

7 May

In certain parts of the world, if people fail to watch over and protect their children, pets and livestock, they run the risk of being devoured by wild animals.

Similarly, if people are careless and fail to protect themselves, then their children and pets – symbolically speaking – will be devoured by wild animals. What are these children and pets? They are your good thoughts and feelings, all your good impulses, all that is synonymous with spiritual wealth, abundance and prosperity. If you truly care about these treasures, you must protect them; otherwise they will be plundered by the dark entities of the astral world. And then you will wonder why you feel destitute and impoverished. Clearly, you have not been vigilant. You have been asleep, and wild animals have come and wreaked havoc...*

* Related reading: *True Alchemy or the Quest for Perfection,* Izvor No. 221, Chap. 4.

8 May

One of the secrets of success is the ability to see. When you leave an office or shop, you should be able to say how many people and how many objects were there, what they were like, exactly where they stood, and so on. Yes, this is important. Not because these details are interesting in themselves, but because it is important to exercise your powers of observation. So many people never notice things!

Ask some men the colour of their wife's eyes: they will be unable to tell you. They have kissed their wife thousands of times but have never noticed the colour of her eyes. Oh yes, there are scatterbrains like that, men and women too, of course. They pass by people and things without seeing them, bumping into them both physically and psychically. Do you think they look before crossing a street? No, not even then; and they go through life with the same lack of attention. Nothing is more important than to learn to see. Whether it be people, things or situations, you must learn to see them.*

* Related reading: *Hrani yoga – The Alchemical and Magical Meaning of Nutrition,* Complete Works Vol. 16, Part II, Chap. VIII.

9 May

We often hear people say, 'I want to be free, I don't want to be influenced by anybody.' But what they do not know is that influence is a law of life. They are constantly being influenced by everything they eat, breathe, touch, taste, hear, see and read. And if they often think that they are free, it is simply because they do not know what influences they are under.

Actually, it is just as well that some people do not know, for if they were aware that they were acting under a good influence, their ridiculous thirst for independence might well lead them to reject it.

10 May

If you isolate a single element to study it, you will never truly understand it, for you will have separated it from the life of the whole. You can understand this single element only if you see how it is linked to all other elements and how life circulates among them.

To know the truth of life, you have to learn to link beings and things with one central idea, and see how they fit into the cosmic edifice in order to see how they participate and vibrate in harmony with universal life. In this way, you will recognize in every individual fact that you study an element that contributes to the maintenance of the whole structure.*

* Related reading: *Truth, Fruit of Wisdom and Love,* Izvor No. 234, Chap. 14.

11 May

So many people do not realize that they are sliding down a dangerous slope. Following, minor frustrations or setbacks, they sink gradually deeper into a morbid state until they are finally engulfed. Something that began as hardly more than a discomfort ends up becoming a catastrophe.

So, be vigilant about your inner states, otherwise some tiny negative element may snowball until it is an immense obstacle on your path, and you find yourself moaning, 'It's in my way; I cannot get round it!' But whose fault is that? Who started this snowball in the first place? You! You have harboured all sorts of negative thoughts and feelings and allowed them to reach gigantic proportions in your head and your heart, and now you are stuck! What can you do about it? Strike a match and hold it close to the snowball, so that the heat melts it. The water will run off and irrigate your gardens and orchards and will give you an abundance of flowers and fruit. That is what you must do: light the fire of love, for love will melt all the tumours within you.*

* Related reading: *Harmony and Health,* Izvor No. 225, Chap. 9.

12 May

*I*nitiatic Science does not teach the occult sciences; it teaches spiritual science. In the occult sciences light and darkness are mixed together, and many occultists who have steeped themselves in the dark regions of these sciences in the hope of using their knowledge to obtain money, women or powers have come to a bad end.

The occult sciences promise a great deal; they tell you that a special perfume, talisman or magic gem will bring you fortune, love and worldly success. Books on the occult abound, and people who are full of lust dabble in them in search of quick and easy ways to satisfy their desires. This is why black magic is so prevalent in the world today. Whereas there are few candidates for the practice of white magic, or theurgy, for very few people have freed themselves from their baser desires and are eager to communicate with the divine world. We must never use esoteric science to satisfy our greed, only to perfect ourselves and help humanity.

13 May

Many of people's conceptions about the Lord need to be reconsidered. The notion of a God who is angry with his people, or of an old man with a long beard busy recording their good and bad deeds and punishing their faults, was perhaps acceptable at one time and under other conditions. But now, frankly, these notions seem ridiculous. No one in their right mind would want anything to do with the life and occupations that have been ascribed to God.

Unquestionably, the notion of one single God, introduced by Moses, represented a great step forward in the history of thought. But there came a time when this image of a harsh, merciless God of justice had to be revised in order for human beings themselves to evolve. For how could they learn to show patience, tolerance and kindness towards their fellow human beings if the example before their eyes was of a God forever intransigent and unforgiving? This is why Jesus came: to bring us the teaching of a God of love.*

* Related reading: *'In Spirit and in Truth'*, Izvor No. 235, Chap. 17.

14 May

Whenever human beings reject all spiritual and moral authority and do as they please, they unwittingly repeat the fault of Adam and Eve. *Genesis* tells us that God placed Adam and Eve in the Garden of Eden and forbade them to eat the fruit of the Tree of the Knowledge of Good and Evil. When they disobeyed they were cast out of the Garden.

The mystery surrounding the Tree of the Knowledge of Good and Evil concerns the forces that are active in nature. Human beings occupy a specific place in the universe and a corresponding level of consciousness that does not allow them to know or experience all that exists with impunity. Although it is true to say that curiosity is one of the main driving forces for human evolution, there are certain experiences for which human beings are still not ready, and to embark on them prematurely is to expose oneself to great dangers. Symbolically speaking, we might say that before the Fall, the first human beings lived among the flowers of the Cosmic Tree, but when they sought to broaden their field of investigation they descended into the roots. There are certainly many things to be discovered among the roots, but Adam and Eve also discovered limitation and death.

15 May

What is a magic wand? It is an instrument that links heaven and earth, that ensures a contact between heaven – the inner psychic world – and earth – the outer, physical world – so that an idea, a wish, an image may be given form and fruition in matter.*

When Jesus pronounced the words of the Lord's Prayer, 'Thy will be done on earth as it is in heaven', he was accomplishing an act of magic, for his words created a link between the higher and the lower worlds. And he asks all human beings to work this magic, to draw down light and purity from above so that the earth becomes a reflection of heaven. The only way to achieve this ideal is to be linked to heaven, to put one's whole being into maintaining this contact with heaven so as to keep the current flowing. A magic wand is like an electrical plug that each one of us must plug in to heaven.

* Related reading: *The Fruits of the Tree of Life – The Cabbalistic Tradition,* Complete Works Vol. 32, Chap. XXI.

16 May

What is a rose, or even a single rose petal? For an Initiate who is versed in the Kabbalah,* it is a means of communication with the world of Venus. Venus belongs to the sephirah *Netzach*, and it was Venus that created the rose. Each rose petal is impregnated with the quintessence of Venus, and through it you can be in contact with the inhabitants and virtues of that region. This petal is imbued with all the quintessence of this region; by looking at it and loving it, you give it some of your magnetism and it gives you something in return, putting you in touch with the inhabitants of Venus, who are more highly evolved than those of Earth. If you need love, tenderness, beauty and perfume, they can be yours, thanks to this petal.

A rose petal is not Venus. You have to go beyond the petal, for it has nothing of its own to give you. Think of it as a channel through which you can communicate with very exalted beings, and they can communicate their gifts to you.

* See plate and note on pp. 398 to 401.

17 May

Look carefully and you will see that those who live in truth stand out from the crowd by reason of all kinds of qualities, particularly their goodness, nobility and altruism. This is why, when I meet someone who claims to possess the truth but who is aggressive, vindictive and full of hatred, I feel like telling them, 'Clear off, old chap, for if that is truth, it is not worth the effort to possess it.' But human beings rarely apply these standards. They hear a rabble-rouser preaching hatred and violence in the name of truth, and they are ready not only to follow them, but to imitate them.

Never believe those who claim to possess truth unless they can show you their diploma. 'There are diplomas for this too?' you will ask. Indeed, but with a difference, for the diploma of those who possess the truth is not printed on a piece of paper, but on a person's very being. It is a living diploma that Initiates and even the spirits of nature can read from afar, for it shines and emits rays of light. When we are in the presence of such a being, we feel an influx of light and warmth, as though we were watching the sun rise.

18 May

*B*roadly speaking, it could be said that the Logos is the synthesis of all the expressions of a person's inner life, of all that emanates from their thoughts and feelings. In this sense, the Logos is often in direct contradiction to a person's words.

Suppose, for instance, that a man detests his neighbour and intends to ruin him; he may set out to lull his victim's misgivings by a great show of friendship, and the poor wretch is taken in by his words. Also, instead of being a truthful reflection of reality, words are often used for no other purpose than to provoke reactions of distrust, hatred, revolt or any other sentiment that the speaker wishes to arouse. So, beware of words! Of course, you might say that most of the time, speech fulfils its magical role, which is to transform reality. True, but it should never be used to transform reality in a negative way. The magical power of speech must be used exclusively for good.*

* Related reading: *The Book of Divine Magic,* Izvor No. 226, Chap. 4.

19 May

Light was the first being created by God. Light is Christ, and Christ is the Cosmic Sun. The spirit of Christ is identical to the solar spirit.* If we learn to unite ourselves to the spirit of the sun, which is the spirit of Christ, an emanation of God himself, He will bless us with gifts of light, warmth, life, beauty, purity, health and so on.

But we cannot obtain all this simply by exposing our body to the sun. Most human beings do this instinctively and without any conscious participation, but that is not enough, for in this way they receive no more than a few rays of sunlight. In order to receive spiritual elements from the sun, our spirit must reach out to touch it, make contact with it, penetrate it, and melt into one with it. Yes, our spirit, not our skin. It is good to expose yourself physically to the sun's rays, but if your consciousness, your intelligence and your spirit participate in the encounter, you will receive far more than heat and vitality: you will receive knowledge, illumination.

* Related reading: *Looking into the Invisible,* Izvor No. 228, Chap. 8.

20 May

*T*he expression 'lifting the veil of Isis' is an image. The 'veil of Isis' is the mystery of living nature that we have not yet unravelled.* And by 'nature', we must also include human beings, for human beings too are shrouded in veils. This is why it is so difficult for human beings to know themselves and each other. True knowledge requires that we rise to the sublime regions of the spirit. Only when we cease to see ourselves and others through the distorting lens of our opaque bodies – for our astral and mental bodies** do not possess true clairvoyance any more than our physical body – shall we at last be able to see the true immensity, light and splendour of human beings on the sublime planes.

All the hierophants of the past shared the same teaching with their disciples, revealing that a human being is a reflection of nature, and both are veiled. Buried beneath the layers of matter dwells a spirit, a spark, an indescribable, omniscient, all-powerful being, God himself. To those who, through asceticism, prayer and sacrifice, are able to obey the demands of the spirit, Isis will reveal herself without her veils.

* Related reading: *'In Spirit and in Truth'*, Izvor No. 235, Chap. 7.

** See note and diagram on pp. 396 and 397.

21 May

*W*hen Jesus came, he taught humans that God was their father, no longer putting the emphasis exclusively on the notion of justice and severity, as Moses had done, but on that of love, kindness and forgiveness. God was no longer portrayed as the unyielding master before whom human beings had to prostrate themselves like slaves. He was a father, and human beings were his children.

This new view of the relationship between human beings and the Lord gave rise to another, even deeper change, which was also mentioned in the Gospels, but which is still not properly understood. This new perspective throws light on the nature of human beings themselves. If God is our father, it means that we are of the same nature as He* – for father and child must necessarily be of the same nature. And if we are of the same nature as God, we can identify with Him; we are in Him and He is in us.

* Related reading: *'In Spirit and in Truth'*, Izvor No. 235, Chap. 17.

22 May

If you look at the glyph of Mercury ☿ , you will notice that the symbols of the Sun and Moon are placed in an unusual position. In principle, as the Sephirotic Tree shows, the Sun is above the Moon – *Tiphareth* is above *Yesod* – and in the hierarchy of the elements, fire is above water. Here, on the contrary, the Sun is below the Moon. Why is this? In order to heat it, to exalt it.

The respective places of Sun and Moon correspond to a cosmic phenomenon, which you will understand more readily if I tell you that it is reproduced in our everyday lives each time you put a kettle of water on the fire to boil. As the water boils it is transformed into steam, which is sometimes strong enough to lift the lid. Fire transforms water into a driving force. Fire represents the masculine principle, and water the feminine principle. So, when the masculine principle acts upon the feminine principle, it produces a force, and Initiates know how to use this force to travel through space. In a human being, the masculine principle is the spirit and the feminine principle is the soul, and when a person's soul, exalted by the spirit, travels through space, that person becomes the perfect incarnation of the symbol of Mercury. This same idea is expressed in Greek mythology, in which the god Hermes (Mercury) is able to fly, thanks to the wings at his heels.

23 May

When the Initiates speak of unity they are not advocating uniformity. They are not saying that we should all have exactly the same thoughts, desires, tastes and activities. Life offers an extraordinarily wide variety of possibilities, and we should look for unity only in the essential aspects.

Human beings are made up of three fundamental principles: mind, heart and will. The mind needs light (knowledge); the heart needs warmth (love); and the will needs to act in an attempt to manifest the light of the mind and the warmth of the heart. It is in this sense that human beings are identical: their basic structure is the same, and their needs and aspirations correspond to that structure. Whether they are aware of this or not, whether they accept the idea or not, this is the truth of their being, and it is in this direction that they must all work.*

* Related reading: 'In Spirit and in Truth', Izvor No. 235, Chap. 5.

24 May

*O*nce upon a time, a man who wanted to be rich made a pact with the devil. 'Very well' said the devil, 'I will bring you money, but you must give me something in return.' 'What would that be?' asked the man. 'Every time I bring you money, you must give me one hair of your head!' replied the devil.* 'Oh, that's nothing,' said the man with relief. Yes, one hair is nothing, but it was not long before he became bald, and this changed many aspects of his life. His fiancée deserted him, saying that he looked ridiculous. In his misery he began to drink and to do all kinds of crazy things, until his friends too deserted him. Then one cold wintry day he went out without a hat, caught cold and died.

Of course, this is just a funny story, but this is how a good many people reason: 'What do I have to lose by cutting my ties with the Lord and satisfying all my whims? Nothing will happen!' Well, unfortunately, something does happen. Every day these people lose a few tiny particles of light and vitality, and as this loss is felt by their family and at work, their whole life gradually changes for the worse.

* Related reading: *Man, Master of his Destiny,* Izvor No. 202, Chap. 5.

25 May

*T*o begin with, we are vulnerable inwardly. Only later do the consequences of this vulnerability gradually manifest themselves externally as well. We see examples of this among doctors and nurses. Those whose faith is very strong and whose blood is pure can live with the victims of plague, leprosy or tuberculosis without being contaminated.* Whereas the germs catch and infect others, even though they try to flee. This is because they have allowed impurities to enter them, and impurities are a fertile ground for microbes and viruses.

The purity of our blood as well as that of our thoughts and feelings is our best defence against illness. But once ill has entered our thoughts and feelings, our hearts and our desires, the door is open, and it can very easily work its way down to the physical plane.

* Related reading: *The Powers of Thought,* Izvor No. 224, Chap. 3.

*O*ur freedom depends on our degree of evolution. This means that for a human being, just as for any other creature, absolute freedom does not exist. Only God the Creator is truly free. Even the angels and archangels, even the cherubim and the seraphim are not absolutely free. All created beings, both angels and humans, are dependent on the Creator, and their degree of freedom is proportionate to their position in the immense hierarchy of beings.

The only way to win our freedom is to turn back to the upward path. How can we do this? By trying to do the will of our Creator. There can be no freedom except in submission to God. When we do His will, God manifests Himself in us, and it is because He is free and because He is within us that we, too, feel free: we are free in His freedom.*

* Related reading: *Freedom, the Spirit Triumphant,* Izvor No. 211.

27 May

*H*ands represent the will. So, if you want to educate your will, begin by getting to know your hands, by educating and caring for them. Know that each finger acts as an antenna that picks up and transmits the different kinds of waves circulating through space. It is because Initiates know how to pick up waves of the purest kind that they can use their hands to work miracles: to soothe and heal, to command the forces of nature.

You should wash your hands frequently so that they can function as perfect antennae.* However, they cannot really be washed by physical water alone. This is why it is a good practice to imagine, as often as you can, that you are turning on a tap of spiritual water, a stream of light of the purest colours and holding your hands under it for as long as possible.

* Related reading: *The Two Trees of Paradise,* Complete Works Vol. 3, Chap. IV.

28 May

Moles live underground, far from the light, and to move around they have to dig long tunnels in the ground, which are sometimes destroyed by a farmer's plough. This dark and limited life probably suits them because they are moles; they can imagine no other.*

The life of a fish is freer than that of a mole; the environment in which fish live and move is lighter and more spacious. But the life of birds is freer still: the wide open spaces are theirs; they are free to sing and rejoice in the sunlight. Moles (earth), fish (water) and birds (air) are symbols that correspond to different levels of consciousness, and it is the level of consciousness that determines destiny.

* Related reading: *Truth, Fruit of Wisdom and Love,* Izvor No. 234, Chap. 18.

29 May

If you want to feel fit and full of joy and hope in the morning, place a good thought in your head before you go to bed at night so that it can work while you are sleeping. Never go to sleep with negative thoughts in your mind, for they will cause all kinds of disorders within you during the night. And if, just before dropping off, you are seized by a sense of anxiety, do not stay in bed, get up, turn on the light, and do a few breathing exercises, say some prayers, or read something uplifting before going back to bed. If the feeling of unease comes back during the night, get up and repeat the process. You cannot defend yourself properly if you are lying down.

There are cases in which the position of the body is very important. You will say, 'But if I get out of bed I'll catch cold. I can defend myself mentally while remaining warm in bed.' No, if you are afraid of catching cold, wrap up warmly, but know that you must be extremely powerful to be able to defend yourself while lying down. We are weaker and more passive in a horizontal position. If you want to defend yourself and dominate the situation, you must get up.*

* Related reading: *A New Earth – Methods, Exercises, Formulas, Prayers,* Complete Works Vol. 13, Chap. II.

30 May

If you want to be happy, open yourself up to others. You will say that the people you meet in the street, in shops and at work are very uninspiring, and that in any case, if you tried to be friendly they would not understand you. That is true; there are some who will not understand. If you smile or greet them warmly, they will think, 'What's got into him? He's not normal!'

But even though a few people are unable to understand you, there are so many who can! Besides, do we live only for the people we meet? No, we live for the whole of creation, visible and invisible, and throughout creation there are hosts of creatures who are capable of appreciating our love. That is what counts.*

* Related reading: *On the Art of Teaching (Part III)*, Complete Works Vol. 29, Chap. VII.

31 May

If men and women lived more sensible, intelligent and purer lives they would become like flowers, for the skin is able to distil a fragrance similar to that of certain flowers that grow only in the mountains.* Long, long ago the first man and woman possessed this scent, particularly Eve, which is why the plants knew and loved her. She communicated with the whole vegetable kingdom, and in Paradise, in the Garden of Eden, no flower exhaled a more exquisite scent than that of Eve. After the original sin – which was a descent into the denser regions of matter – Eve lost her ability to distil this perfume, and the flowers no longer recognized her. For flowers are pure and chaste. They have no astral desires, and when they saw how Eve had sinned, they stopped sharing their virtues with her.

It is because women still have the subconscious memory of their former condition in Paradise that they feel the need to wear perfume. They should know that even now they could still recover that scent if they regained their original state of purity through pure food, pure feelings and pure thoughts.

* Related reading: *'In Spirit and in Truth'*, Izvor No. 235, Chap. 10.

1 June

People sometimes complain, 'Since I decided to change my way of life and follow a spiritual teaching, I have been miserable.' But were they really happy before? No, I do not think so. On the face of it, yes, perhaps, because those who never exert themselves are seemingly at peace. All the while, the impurities resulting from a disordered life accumulate within them, and at some point they sense that something is wrong – they become anxious or depressed and fall ill.

On the other hand, those who decide to introduce purity and light* into their psychic life may at first experience some unpleasantness from the revolution they have set in motion within themselves, but once this period is over, they find peace, freedom and happiness. This is what we must understand. In the first case, despite a semblance of tranquillity, ruin is already in the making. Those who do not live properly can always say, 'I feel fine, I'm doing well', but in reality they are mistaken; it is like a beautiful house whose beams have already been eaten away by worms. It may still be solid for the moment, but one day...

* Related reading: *The Wellsprings of Eternal Joy*, Izvor No. 242, Chap. 17.

2 June

When we open our window in the morning and get a glimpse of the sun, we are happy to see its light, feel its warmth, and soak up the life that it spreads throughout the universe. But if we could rise above the earth and get closer to the sun, we might find something dark and obscure that would not make us happy at all. This is a mystery that needs to be explored further.

In ancient Egypt, when a disciple attained the ultimate degree of initiation, the high priest would whisper in his ear, 'Osiris is a black god. Osiris is darkness, three times darkness.' How could Osiris, the god of light and of the sun, be black? The disciple was troubled by this, for darkness symbolizes evil and the unknowable.* Could he have sought light, have run the full course, only to discover darkness? The reality is that Osiris is so luminous that he seems dark. He is the light beyond all light.

* Related reading: *Angels and other Mysteries of The Tree of Life,* Izvor No. 236, Chap. 6.

3 June

The Initiates have left traces of their presence in the etheric matter of the places where they once lived. Certain highly evolved clairvoyants are able to perceive these traces and interpret them. But even such traces are no more than husks of the spirit that once breathed in this place. There is really no guarantee that one will find the spirit by visiting the place where it once breathed.*

'Then how can we communicate with the spirits of the great Initiates of India, Egypt, Chaldea, Israel or Greece?' you will ask. In reality, they are not dead; they have gone back to their homeland, the sun. Yes, all those luminous spirits who once came to enlighten the world have returned to live in the sun from where they came, and they continue to help us from up above. It is through the sun's rays that they communicate with us, smile on us, caress, purify and vivify us. These rays are, as it were, their arms and their hands but their spirit remains on high. If you learn to follow the traces of the sun's rays you will eventually reach their spirit.

* Related reading: 'In Spirit and in Truth', Izvor No. 235, Chap. 13.

4 June

Water is composed of two gases, oxygen and hydrogen, and in order for these two gases to combine and produce water, the intervention of fire is necessary. As soon as a spark is lit, the two gases burn with an eternal love for each other and become one. They do not give birth to a third gas but to a liquid, which represents a different state of matter. So, a new element enters the equation, triggering a fusion that is accompanied by a change in state. Oxygen and hydrogen are invisible, intangible and volatile, whereas water can be seen, touched and even kept in a container.

Now, if you heat water, it becomes steam and disappears. On the other hand, if you chill it sufficiently, it solidifies and becomes ice. The saga of water raises some interesting questions. For instance, shouldn't what is true for water be equally true for all other substances? Or, again, since water can exist in the three different states – solid, liquid and gaseous, which correspond to the elements earth, water, and air – mustn't it also exist in an etheric form, which corresponds to the element fire?*

* Related reading: *The Mysteries of Fire and Water,* Izvor No. 232.

5 June

Music, true music such as it is understood by the Initiates, is not just the audible arrangement of sounds created by human beings. When Initiates speak of the 'music of the spheres',* they are referring to the harmony that reigns between all the elements of the universe, to an order, an arrangement, based on the relationships of numbers.

Harmony is primarily a structure; only when it descends to the material plane does it create forms. In this sense, harmony is the expression of divine reason and wisdom, and this is why it is also identified with the divine Word, the Logos. Harmony and music can exist only in the presence of reason and wisdom. The divine Word, music and wisdom, are one and the same.

* Related reading: *Angels and other Mysteries of The Tree of Life,* Izvor No. 236, Chap. 3.

6 June

*E*verybody knows how inconvenient blocked pipes, dirty windows or smeared eyeglasses can be. Very few, however, realize that they are harbouring these same inconveniences within themselves, in the form of thoughts, feelings and desires that are like stains, dust and trash, which block up their spiritual channels and prevent divine light from reaching and entering them. You can build nothing solid or durable in the spiritual life unless you begin by purifying yourself.

Why do you suppose that all religions attach so much importance to purity? Simply for its own sake, and nothing beyond that? No, they insist on purity because it is the foundation of all spiritual life, and the function of a foundation is to bear the weight of the whole edifice. Purity is the prerequisite that must be met before we can begin to learn and create in the spiritual world.*

* Related reading: *The Mysteries of Yesod,* Complete Works Vol. 7.

7 June

If you work seriously and in depth to purify yourself, light will flow into you more and more readily, and you will begin to see things more clearly and with greater lucidity. The sickly particles in your body will be eliminated and your physical health will begin to improve; those that hamper your willpower will also be driven out and you will become stronger. All that is dark and shadowy will leave you, and if you were sad, you will find yourself filled with joy. For joy is simply an aspect of purity: the more you purify yourself, the more light-hearted, gay and joyful you will feel.

And just as impurity leads to fermentation, putrefaction, disintegration and death, the exact opposite happens when you purify yourself: you draw closer to immortality. So, health, power, knowledge, happiness and immortality are simply different aspects of purity. This, in short, is the whole of Initiatic Science; it is now up to you to verify it.*

* Related reading: *The Mysteries of Yesod,* Complete Works Vol. 7.

8 June

When you sing or pray together, any misunderstandings between you disappear. Prayer and song are magical powers, capable of dispelling the darkness. This is why you must never miss an opportunity to do this work together, to acquire this new consciousness: the consciousness of unity.

In a spiritual brotherhood, you will find the conditions you need to learn to create true peace and harmony. So, instead of wandering off in all directions in search of distractions that will help you to forget your cares and sorrows or the difficulties you experience with others, you would do far better to come and join them to sing and pray with them. Little by little, a new order, a new purity, a liberation and illumination will begin to reign within you. This is how, all together, you will be preparing a nucleus of the new life.

9 June

You must do more than picture yourself surrounded by colours to form your aura, for those colours cannot last if they are not nurtured and maintained by the practice of the virtues of which they are the material expression. It is the virtues that nourish the colours of our aura.

When the spirits of the higher worlds look towards the earth, they often see nothing but darkness. But when they see just one luminous being radiating beams of light in the midst of that darkness, they come to protect and care for that person.

10 June

If you are willing to help others and put up with the difficulties this involves, other beings of a higher order will decide to help and support you. As long as you refuse to have anything to do with those who are in an inferior position, you will be depriving yourself of certain exchanges with them, and the invisible world, in turn, will refuse to exchange with you.

It is important for human beings to learn to have genuinely reciprocal relationships. The wise and learned must pass on their light, and the ignorant must receive it and rejoice in it. The rich must visit the poor and be happy that they are able to do some good; the poor should feel helped and encouraged. Such sincere, brotherly reciprocity is a source of great happiness. But those whose granaries and coffers are full and who refuse to put their wealth into circulation become like swamps: they maintain a state of inner stagnation. They will never discover the meaning of life for they fail to recognize the powerful law of reciprocity.*

* Related reading: *Cosmic Balance, The Secret of Polarity,* Izvor No. 237, Chap. 12.

11 June

Do not allow division within yourself by entertaining several different thoughts or contradictory desires at the same time, but rather work to create unity by trusting in the Lord.* 'Unity' means that all the parts at the periphery converge towards the centre. Only then is it possible to act effectively.

No living creature – whether a single atom or a human being – can subsist unless all its elements, even those on the farthest fringe, are organized round a single centre. Observe what goes on in life, and you will see that division, dichotomy, leads to much suffering and failure, whereas unity leads to success. Your happiness and success, even your health, will always depend on your efforts to attain unity.

* Related reading: *Man, Master of his Destiny,* Izvor No. 202, Chap. 5.

12 June

*T*he venerable being who addresses St John in *Revelation* declares, *'I am the Alpha and the Omega, the First and the Last, the Beginning and the End.'* Alpha and omega are the first and last letters of the Greek alphabet, the language in which the New Testament was written. In Hebrew, which was the language Jesus spoke, the first and last letters of the alphabet are aleph and tav.

Alpha and omega, or aleph and tav… To speak of these two letters is to speak of the whole alphabet, for the first cannot be isolated from the last. An alphabet is a whole formed of a number of elements – the letters – and the order in which the letters follow each other is not random. They are the analogical representation of the 'letters' that exist in creation. The letters of the Hebrew alphabet represent the elements, forces, virtues, qualities, spirits and powers, which God combined in order to create the universe. By means of these living letters, God formed words and sentences, and He continues to form words and sentences. This is how the world was created and continues to be created.

13 June

*M*atter restricts and imprisons us. It is an obstacle between us and the spiritual world, which was not meant to paralyze or bury us under mounds of rubble, but to oblige us to carry out special work on it. For those who moan, 'I feel so limited and shackled. How did I ever get into this mess? And how can I get out of it?' there is only one answer: work with love, wisdom and willpower. Get back on the upward path. Do not wait to be completely incapacitated.

Picture someone wading in a pool of cement: as long as it is still wet he can step out of it. But if he is absent-minded and starts thinking of something else, the cement will harden and he will be trapped. Now the cement will have to be broken apart at the risk of hurting him.* Yes, this is how it is: time hardens things, and if you delay getting out of certain states, you will soon be permanently stuck. When you abandon yourself to the comforts and pleasures of the material world, you distance yourself from the divine world and, all too often, the very things in which you expected to find freedom and happiness bring you only servitude and suffering.

---

* Related reading: *'Know Thyself' – Jnana Yoga (Part I),* Complete Works Vol. 17, Chap. IX.

14 June

You believe yourselves to be free simply because you are in a position to do as you like. Yet, if you analyze yourselves, you will see that many of your choices are dictated by certain overriding instincts, desires or appetites, which you cannot resist. Your freedom is therefore more apparent than real.

How valiantly human beings have fought to be free! Even death has often seemed preferable to the loss of freedom. What a pity that they have never made the same efforts or fought so courageously to be spiritually free. They are interested only in external freedom; their inner enslavement does not bother them. Those who are in a position to satisfy all their basest tendencies think that they are free. No, it is precisely in this instance that they are slaves.*

* Related reading: *Freedom, the Spirit Triumphant,* Izvor No. 211.

15 June

Among the thousands of things human beings need to understand, there is one in particular that they have neglected, and that is the question of attitude; the attitude they should have towards nature, towards other human beings, and towards the Creator. Yes, especially towards the Creator. Instead of turning to him, as the needle of a compass turns to the North Star, people turn their backs on Him. This is why they encounter so many difficulties and trials.

This question of attitude is essential, for it determines the whole of our inner and outer life. We should try every day to adopt the right attitude towards this pole star that we call God, so that we may receive all blessings from Him. And once we have the right attitude towards God, we shall also find the right attitude towards all other creatures, other human beings, the whole of nature.*

* Related reading: *Youth: Creators of the Future,* Izvor No. 233, Chap. 3.

16 June

Conventional science is still a long way from understanding how God created human beings in His heavenly workshops. Only the greatest clairvoyants and Initiates have been able to see the reality of something so remote, and they tell us that in their essence, human beings are actually without form. They consist of currents of energy and luminous emanations, and those currents and emanations have gradually condensed to form the physical organs we know today.

So, our stomach, liver, spleen, brain, eyes, ears, legs and arms are the materialization of forces that flow on a subtler plane. When human beings behave unreasonably, it is as though they were gradually extinguishing their lights – that is, their virtues and forces – on these higher planes, and then the organs that correspond to those virtues and forces begin to fail. This explains people's physical health problems: they fall ill because their lights dim and go out on high.*

* Related reading: *Love and Sexuality (Part I)*, Complete Works Vol. 14, Chap. III.

17 June

If you really want something, you can impose your will even on God. Yes, if you know how to wrestle with him, the victory can be yours. Are you suffering and under stress? Do you have the feeling that God has abandoned you, or that he wants to crush you? So turn to him and say, 'Lord, you have declared war on me. You want to strike me down, but I will not give in. I'm going to fight you.'

How can you fight God? With the very same weapons that he uses. Since God is love, you must fight using the arms of love. Draw near to him, put your arms round his neck, and tell him, 'I love you, Lord. You can do what you like with me, I accept it.' Then the Lord will scratch his head and say to himself, 'What am I to do about this child? I cannot go on making him suffer'. He will think on it, embrace you, and your battle will be over. You will once again dwell in his peace and light. This is how you can defeat the Lord: through love.*

* Related reading: *On the Art of Teaching (Part III),* Complete Works Vol. 29, Chap. VII, Parts II and III.

18 June

Everything that exists in the universe is made of threads, of ties. Even our physical body is a network of threads and connections that we call fibres, filaments, nerves, canals, vessels, plexuses or tissues.

If you were clairvoyant, you would also see that human beings are entangled in multiple ties that spread out from them on every side. And yet they imagine that they are all separate from one another, all free and independent. No, the mere fact of thinking of others links you to them, for thoughts are ties, threads. If you wish to do someone harm, your thoughts are like a rope, a lasso that you throw to catch and destroy them. On the other hand, if you love somebody very much, your thoughts will be a conduit through which you can nourish them, a link that you create between them and all that is best, in order to help and enlighten them. All thoughts and feelings, whether inspired by love or hatred, are links.*

* Related reading: *Love and Sexuality (Part I),* Complete Works Vol. 14, Chap. XXV.

19 June

Learn to be lucid about what goes on inside you. You must seek not only to identify your desires, feelings and thoughts, but also to recognize whether they stem from your higher or your lower nature. You should even try to discern their colour and scent, and know the nature of the entities to which they correspond. For everything has a specific place and belongs to a specific category. Everything we experience in our consciousness is a reflection of either the higher world or the lower world.

That which we call consciousness can in fact be an expression of unconsciousness, the subconscious or the superconscious; it just depends on what is active and projected on the screen of our consciousness. Dark manifestations are the expression of the subconscious, whereas luminous manifestations are an expression of the superconscious. Our consciousness is a neutral zone in which both good and evil can manifest, and our first duty is to learn to distinguish between the two.*

* Related reading: *'Know Thyself' – Jnana Yoga (Part I),* Complete Works Vol. 17, Chap. VII.

20 June

*H*uman beings possess two kinds of knowledge: that which truly belongs to them, and that which is somewhat alien to them. Those whose knowledge is purely theoretical and never put into practice in life are not really the owners of that knowledge. Even if they are considered to be the greatest philosophers on earth, they will be obliged to return as ignorant men or women in their next reincarnation, deprived of all the knowledge they once had. Whereas the humblest human beings who strive to put what they know of the virtues into practice will return with innate possibilities, with true intelligence and wisdom.

All the knowledge that you have lived and experienced for yourselves will remain yours, and you will take it with you, even if you live on another planet one day. But your theoretical knowledge, all that you have learned from books, will fade and be lost, for it is only borrowed.*

* Related reading: *Education Begins Before Birth,* Izvor No. 203, Chap. 11.

21 June

A human being's greatest wealth is the faculty of creation. It is a faculty that concerns every aspect of life, particularly art. But artists need to ask themselves about the value of what they create, what it can do for others, what it will lead to – they must think about this too.

They tell you that they feel the need to get something out of their system, to express themselves. Well, everybody needs to get something out of their system in one way or another, but is it really necessary to put it all on display? Unfortunately, in the field of art, literature or philosophy, that is what a great many creators do: they present their excrement to the public. You will say that I am exaggerating. No, it is no exaggeration! Artists need to return to the conception of art that was once taught in initiatic schools and produce only works of art that inspire the human soul and help it to find the way back to its celestial homeland.

22 June

You want life to be smooth and pleasant, without problems or unhappiness. But why don't you ask yourself about the underlying meaning of the obstacles that exist in nature and in life instead?

If the path up a high mountain were smooth, you would never be able to climb to the top in order to breathe the pure air and admire the beautiful view, because you would have nothing to cling to. You would keep sliding down to the bottom of the precipice. This is what happens to those whose life is too easy, too comfortable: they lose their grip on life – as well as on their fortune, their health, even their sanity. Since you are climbing up the slopes of a spiritual mountain, do not ask that they be smooth. Be grateful for the rough edges, for it is they that give you a handhold and enable you to keep advancing towards the light.*

* Related reading: *The Mysteries of Fire and Water,* Izvor No. 232, Chap. 7.

Imagine a man who is very dynamic, hot-headed and even violent. He is so curt and emphatic that he can hardly open his mouth without angering, offending or wounding other people. His impulsive temperament leads to these outbursts and causes damage.

Then, one day, finally realizing that such an attitude is extremely detrimental, he takes himself in hand and, after a while, by dint of willpower, he manages to be more moderate and conciliatory, and his life begins to change. Fundamentally, he is the same. He is still quite capable of hitting out with his words or his fists – and this will be true to the end of his days – but thanks to his strength of will he manages to control himself. Unfortunately, too few are willing to undertake such efforts, and yet it is absolutely vital for you to learn to control and master yourselves, and to find just the right gesture, word or expression that will do no damage.*

* Related reading: *Life Force,* Complete Works Vol. 5, Chap. II.

24 June

*T*he feast of St John, which comes just as the Sun enters Cancer, is not a celebration of spiritual fire but of physical, earthly fire. And this fire is not only that which ripens the wheat and the fruit on the trees, but also the inner fire of the planet that maintains a great body of molten matter in which minerals and metals are elaborated. This fire has often been identified with the fires of hell.

In certain traditions, summer is symbolized by a fire-breathing dragon. The dragon is the mythical monster that lives underground and appears on the surface only in order to burn, devour and destroy. But it is also the guardian of all hidden treasure – precious stones and metals – the fruits of the earth, and those who wish to obtain these treasures must be able to face the dragon and defeat it. Here too, many traditions, which often come down to us in the form of fairy tales, tell of the daring hero who conquers the dragon and takes possession of its treasures. Disciples would do well to meditate on such tales: the fact that the summer releases subterranean forces is no reason to let ourselves be devoured by the dragon.*

* Related reading: *Angels and other Mysteries of the Tree of Life,* Izvor No. 236, Chap. 12.

25 June

When human beings incarnate on earth, they begin by spending nine months in the womb in which they are linked to their mother by the umbilical cord. After nine months, this cord must be cut so that they may live their own life as individuals. It is at this point that we say a person is born. But in order to go on living, humans still have to be linked to the universe by a more tenuous, fluidic cord, and the day this cord is cut, they die. Finally, there is a third, even subtler cord that links us to God.

It is this cord that many people cut in their minds, and although they may say, 'We are alive, as you can well see', the truth is that they are dead. Something essential within them has died. Having severed their link with the source of divine light and warmth, they drift away and lose themselves in the cold and dark. They are spiritually dead. They may still be alive on the physical plane, because they have not yet cut the umbilical cord that ties them to Mother Nature, but on the spiritual level they are dead, and this spiritual death inevitably has repercussions on every aspect of their existence.*

* Related reading: *Man's Subtle Bodies and Centres,* Izvor No. 219, Chap. 3.

26 June

All human beings must love, but they should not confine their love to their husband or wife. They must love all men and women. Some people may say, 'Are you urging us to be unfaithful to our spouse?' Oh dear, as if you needed any urging! Be honest: can you truthfully say that you have never loved another man or woman? Can you deny that many a face seen in passing has crept into your heart and soul where you treasure them? Is this wrong? No, on the contrary, but on condition that while remaining faithful, you do not restrict yourself to those few, but consciously let your love embrace the whole world.

Only an immense, rich, pure love such as this can make you happy and bring happiness to the one with whom you share your life. And you must also allow your partner the same freedom to love. In this way you, too, will be the beneficiary of a richer, more beautiful, more luminous love.*

* Related reading: *Love and Sexuality (Part II),* Complete Works Vol. 15, Chap. XXI.

27 June

*E*very activity, whether physical, emotional, or intellectual, involves combustion, and combustion produces waste. Well, these wastes must be discarded, for if they accumulate in the body, they prevent it from functioning properly.

When you want to light a fire in a stove or a hearth, you begin by clearing out yesterday's cinders and ashes, otherwise your fire will not draw well, and the stove will not work. The same applies to your physical body, but equally to your psychic body, to your thoughts and feelings. This is why you must have not only good physical hygiene, but you must also keep an eye on the quality of your thoughts and feelings, so that they produce the least possible amount of waste in your psychic bodies. In this way, you can feed your inner fire and be able to continue your work.*

* Related reading: *Light is a Living Spirit,* Izvor No. 212, Chap. 7.

28 June

What does it mean to say that somebody is naked? One of two things: either that they are poor, deprived, without qualities or virtues; or that having stripped away the shell that prevented light and truth from entering, they are innocent, free and perfect.

In this sense, only those who are truly divine are naked; such beings are also said to be enveloped or clothed in light. It is very difficult to find words that convey an exact notion of the realities of the spiritual life. We are often obliged to have recourse to analogies, and that of nudity serves to express both spiritual poverty and spiritual wealth.*

* Related reading: *The Living Book of Nature,* Izvor No. 216, Chap. 7.

29 June

In the *Book of Exodus* it is written that when God entrusted Moses with the mission of freeing the Hebrews from the Egyptian yoke, Moses replied: *'If I come to the Israelites and say to them, "The God of your ancestors has sent me to you," and they ask me, "What is his name?" what shall I say to them?'* Then God replied: *'Ehyeh Asher Ehyeh'* (the literal meaning of which is 'I will be who I will be'). And God added: *'Thus you shall say to the Israelites: "I will be" has sent me to you.'*

God names Himself 'I will be' in order to show that He is not fully manifested. He is the Being of sublime becoming, He whom we can neither see, nor hear, nor touch.*

* Related reading: *Angels and other Mysteries of The Tree of Life,* Izvor No. 236, Chap. 4.

30 June

*T*he universe is like a tree. In fact, in many religious traditions the Cosmic Tree is a symbol of Creation. Depending on their degree of evolution, human beings dwell in either the roots, the trunk or the branches of this tree.

The roots absorb elements from the earth; its leaves absorb light from the sun, which transforms the raw sap into the vital cell sap; its colourful, fragrant flowers prepare to become fruit, and the fruit not only provides nourishment for animals and people, it also contains the seeds from which other trees will be born. Roots, trunk and branches are all useful and beautiful in their own way, but who would not prefer to live in the branches of a tree, amongst the leaves, flowers and fruit, which are exposed to the light and warmth of the sun?*

* Related reading: *Truth, Fruit of Wisdom and Love,* Izvor No. 234, Chap. 18.

1 July

Life on earth is like a ball that has lost some of its air, and it has been like that ever since it was punctured by the first sin. Many people have tried to reflate that ball, but as soon as they manage to correct the dent on one side, it appears on the other. Why? Because there is not enough air inside the ball. So how can we solve this problem and make the ball round again?

Physical life is analogous to patching the hole in the ball, and spiritual life is analogous to pumping more air into it. So, if we organize only our material life and forget about the spiritual life, or if we think only about the spiritual side and completely neglect the material, the ball will never regain its perfect shape. From now on, each of us must begin by blowing air into our own deflated ball – our earthly existence – and this air is faith, hope and love.*

* Related reading: *The Two Trees of Paradise,* Complete Works Vol. 3, Chap. IX, Part II.

2 July

A very rich man should take care not to make his fortune too obvious to his children, because if it is, they will rely on their future inheritance and make no effort to work or learn to fend for themselves. They will become lazy and capricious, and that is the worst upbringing of all. As much as possible, parents should leave their children in ignorance of the riches that are in store for them. They should speak about it only when their children have developed good work habits and self-mastery. Not before.

That is how God treats us human beings. The Lord is the supreme educator, the most skilful teacher. He does not immediately show us signs of the wealth that awaits us on high. So we work and struggle because we think we are poor and miserable. And when, with suffering and tears, we at last prove ourselves to be worthy of our celestial inheritance, our Father shows us all the treasure He has amassed for us.

3 July

Young people sometimes tell me about their plans to choose a job that will bring in a lot of money because, they add, this will allow them to help others. Do you imagine that I am impressed by their words? Well no, not at all, for I can always see something highly personal lurking behind these seemingly generous intentions.

Those who speak in this way do not know what they are getting caught up in, and once they have taken that first step, their whole being will gradually be drawn in. When earning a lot of money starts to be your goal, be aware that you are burrowing down into matter and that one day you will be so engulfed by it, not only will you soon forget that you wanted to help others, but you will become selfish and hard as well. Yes, we are full of good intentions, but matter is a trap for the children of God. 'So what should we do?' you will ask. 'Must we give up on achieving material success?' No, but first you should spend years strengthening yourself spiritually; only then can you seek material success without fear of losing your way.*

---

* Related reading: *The Seeds of Happiness,* Izvor No. 231, Chap. 1.

4 July

When the Mysteries were celebrated in the temples of Antiquity, Initiates watched young virgins perform sacred dances. These girls devoted their whole lives to purity and were not allowed to show themselves to the uninitiated. Others – disciples who were expelled from the temples because of their weaknesses – wished to imitate them, and set up schools offering so-called 'initiation' into the great mysteries. But when we are not sufficiently elevated to contemplate celestial beauty, we make do with crude imitations.

That is why, nowadays, the people who cram into strip-clubs to catch a glimpse of 'Isis unveiled' are none other than those disciples of the past who, having failed their true initiatic tests, now return to these sordid places for another try. Here, they all receive their diplomas with flying colours, because this 'Isis' unveils herself much more readily than the goddess of the ancient temples! What a pity, for those who know how to contemplate true beauty can rise to the very throne of God.

5 July

*T*o seek pleasure is a normal tendency in every human being – we all know that. However, should we have absolute faith in this natural impulse that urges us to satisfy all our instinctive desires? Some people enjoy eating or drinking to excess, others take pleasure in fighting, stealing, vandalizing or seducing women.

It is easy to understand why they find these things pleasant, for nature offers such a wealth of possibilities. But this tendency to indulge in pleasure cannot be completely justified unless it is directed and controlled by the presence of wisdom and reason. The basic impulse is permissible, but never such manifestations; it must not be allowed to run free and out of control. All needs are wonderful forces; there is nothing wrong with them. It is only when the other factor – the guiding words of wisdom – is absent that these instincts become harmful.*

* Related reading: *Truth, Fruit of Wisdom and Love,* Izvor No. 234, Chap. 1.

6 July

*E*veryone knows that you need a guide to climb the peaks of high mountains. In the world of sports, everybody recognizes the usefulness and even the necessity of a guide. But when it comes to their inner life, many people think they have no need of a guide. In the inner life, we are much more at risk of getting lost, of being crushed in avalanches or of falling over precipices, and yet it is quite extraordinary how many people think they can get along on their own, without a guiding hand. Yes, that is the reason we come across so many sick, unbalanced and mentally disturbed people: they did not want a guide and got lost in their inner maze.*

* Related reading: *Life and Work in an Initiatic School – Training for the Divine,* Complete Works Vol. 30, Chap. III.

7 July

There was a time when people were truly capable of loving each other and staying faithful, a time when the institution of marriage did not exist. The custom of marriage was instituted because people no longer knew how to love. Laws, sacraments, and so on, had to be invented to bind them together.

Is there any need for documents, contracts, a mayor or a priest when there is love? In any case, these mayors, priests and contracts do not prevent couples from tearing each other apart and separating. When there is love, nothing else is needed for it to last forever, not even the blessing of a priest, because God has already given His blessing. God is present within the love of those who truly love each other, and that is the real blessing: love itself.*

* Related reading: *Cosmic Creation, Union of the Masculine and Feminine,* Izvor No. 214, Chap. 3.

8 July

When a teacher has finished with his classes, he dismisses his students and returns to his personal occupations, thoughts, feelings and problems. He has delivered his lesson and that is the end of it. A spiritual master, on the other hand, never stops looking after his disciples: day and night, when he eats, when he works and when he sleeps he is caring for their souls and spirits. In this way, he constantly helps them every single day.

You may ask yourself how this is possible. Well, it is simply that an Initiate is free. And when we are free, when we have resolved all our personal problems, then we can help our friends, disciples and students. Whereas, if we are always too caught up and embroiled in our own affairs (as most people are), what can we do for other people? This is yet another difference between a true spiritual master and an ordinary instructor.*

* Related reading: *What is a Spiritual Master?*, Izvor No. 207.

9 July

Money is the source of all sorts of temptations. You need great strength to lead the same spiritual life in the midst of opulence as you would with just the bare necessities.

Why do you suppose that hermits go to live in the desert, and monks take a vow of poverty? Because wealth does not provide the best conditions for the spiritual life, which demands so much inner discipline and renunciation. Hermits and monks have understood that their true wealth lies in peace and clarity of vision. For what sort of wealth is obtained at the expense of all our most precious inner assets? True wealth is the wealth of good thoughts and feelings that we can distribute to everybody, without ever emptying our coffers.*

* Related reading: *A New Dawn: Society and Politics in the Light of Initiatic Science (Part I)*, Complete Works Vol. 25, Chap. VI.

10 July

*T*he spirits of darkness are wily. They do not appear before you with horns, a forked tail, surrounded by all the cauldrons of hell, because they do not wish to frighten you. On the contrary, they come with the promise that all your wishes will be granted, and they persist again and again, until, like an overripe fruit, you fall into their snares. That is how they manage to seduce people: by promising power, pleasure and money.

The spirits of good, on the other hand, say, 'If you listen to us, you may not gain fame or fortune, because the Prince of this World is the guardian of these things. But we can offer you other things: light, peace, knowledge and above all, abundant life. Would you like to join us?' If you are enlightened and truly discerning, you will listen to the voices of the heavenly spirits; if you do not, of course, you will fall into the traps laid for you by the spirits of darkness.*

* Related reading: *The True Meaning of Christ's Teaching,* Izvor No. 215, Chap. 9.

11 July

*F*rom an anatomical and physiological point of view, the human brain represents the pinnacle of organization. However, this does not mean that everybody is well organized psychologically: it is obvious that people's thoughts and feelings are constantly muddled, contradictory and colliding. And is society well organized? On the face of it, yes, everything works well – water, electricity, gas, cars, trains, the postal service, the police, hospitals, and so on. But this organization is merely mechanical, because the harmony that is integral to the notion of organization is still missing.

In reality, the word 'organization' can apply only to the divine world, where everything functions smoothly and without discord. On earth, when we talk about 'perfect organization', 'an organized mind' or a 'well-organized society', we refer only to physical, material organization: in fact, disorder still reigns in the psychic or spiritual realm.*

* Related reading: *A New Dawn: Society and Politics in the Light of Initiatic Science (Part II),* Complete Works Vol. 26, Chap. IV.

12 July

When we go to buy something in a shop, we must give something in exchange for what we want, do we not? If we do not want to pay, we will not be given anything.

The same thing applies in nature and in the invisible world. The invisible world says, 'Give your heart to God and He will give you everything in return.' But you reply, 'I can't – I have already given my heart to my wife, my children, my adorable mistress, and I have nothing left to give.' Yes, and that is why your prayers are never answered. You always imagine you can obtain something without giving anything in exchange, but that is impossible. To obtain blessings from heaven, you must at least give a part of your love, your conscious attention, your time and your daily efforts.

13 July

It is the nature of your needs that determines your destiny. For example, if you need large quantities of cigarettes or alcohol each day, if you need to accumulate possessions (houses, cars or businesses), or if you need to spend your evenings in nightclubs or playing roulette at the casino, your destiny is already laid out for you: moral decay, ruin, possibly even prison. And if your need is to contemplate divine beauty or spread peace and light all around, your destiny is equally clear: happiness and fulfilment will come your way.

How is it that people do not realize that each need, wish and desire places them on set tracks leading either to regions infested with wasps, snakes and wild beasts from which they will not come back alive, or else toward light-filled, magnificent regions, where they will find untold joy? According to our inclinations, tastes and desires, it is we ourselves who determine our eventual destination.*

* Related reading: *Man, Master of his Destiny,* Izvor No. 202.

14 July

We need solid nourishment to survive on the physical plane. However, in the invisible world, there are creatures who obtain nourishment only from perfumes, colours and sounds.

The majority of people find it difficult to accept that beyond the realms of minerals, plants, animals and human beings, there exist regions they cannot see, inhabited by creatures totally different from anything they know. In fact, the whole universe is filled with the most extraordinary creatures, some of whom nourish themselves with light, colours and sounds. Very advanced human beings have visited these creatures. Of course, for us, colours, music and light are not very substantial foods, but for these entities, formed as they are of such subtle, tenuous matter, light, sounds and perfumes represent not only strength and power but also nourishment.*

* Related reading: *The Tree of the Knowledge of Good and Evil,* Izvor No. 210, Chap. 6.

15 July

You can work on your aura in two ways. By means of thought and imagination, you can strive to attract the purest, most beautiful colours and surround yourself with them. Be aware, however, that this method will bring short-lived, even artificial results, unless at the same time you work on the qualities corresponding to these colours. For what is most essential is to develop our virtues rather than exercise our brains.

Even if you never use thought to form the colours of your aura, and concentrate solely on developing divine virtues within you, all the corresponding colours will come to you in all their beauty, whether you like it or not. As long as you continue to work on these virtues, the colours of your aura will shine out with ever more beauty and brilliance.

16 July

Whether they belong to the mineral, vegetable, animal or human realm, all creatures are conscious but, depending on their degree of evolution, this consciousness is more or less removed from their physical bodies.

The consciousness of minerals is the furthest removed, and this is why they exist in an inert state. The consciousness of plants is at the centre of the earth, so that is where we must try to reach them if we want to speak to them, and get them to understand us and respond. Animals do not have an individual consciousness either: their collective consciousness lies apart from them, within the group soul that directs each different species. Each animal obeys the group soul of its species, which determines the season for mating, for egg laying, for migration, for moulting, and so forth. Humans are the only beings who possess an individual consciousness, and that is why we are thinking beings endowed with free will.*

* Related reading: 'Know Thyself' – Jnana Yoga (Part I), Complete Works Vol. 17, Chap. VII.

17 July

For disciples, adaptability means opening up, having intuition and tact, sensing the right word to say and the right moment to say it, knowing the best time for action, and finally, finding the right attitude. But all this must be accomplished without ever losing sight of their ideal, and without compromising the spiritual principles of honesty, uprightness and integrity. Understood in this way, adaptability calls for strength of character and a subtle intelligence.

Their convictions must remain firm and unshakeable, but at the same time, disciples must demonstrate their ability to be adaptable. Even when cut into pieces, true servants of God remain steadfast in their love and faith.*

* Related reading: *Life and Work in an Initiatic School – Training for the Divine,* Complete Works Vol. 30.

18 July

Banks exist in heaven, just as they do on earth. Without our knowing, all our most pure and luminous emanations, all our acts, feelings and thoughts inspired by noble ideals, unselfishness and generosity are classified by beings whose job it is to do so. They then credit our accounts in these heavenly banks accordingly, thus building up our divine capital. Later, when we go through difficult times, or when we want to do good and offer help to others, we can ask this bank for assistance, and our request will be granted immediately. But if no capital has been deposited there, this heavenly bank will not recognize us.

Many people wonder if heaven has heard their prayers. The answer is that heaven only listens to and fulfils the requests of those who have placed capital in this divine bank.*

* Related reading: *New Light on the Gospels,* Izvor No. 217, Chap. 4.

19 July

If you feel that your meditations and prayers are all for nothing, or next to nothing, it is because you are aiming for the heights without first getting rid of your old, thick, rough clothes – symbolically speaking. What can you expect your soul to receive in such conditions?

Heaven's light and answers are unable to reach you; they cannot get through that shell. You must remove it and present yourself before heaven wearing light, transparent garments, that is, work to rid yourself of selfish schemes and desires, mistaken ideas and pettiness. Once you have managed to do this, the moment you close your eyes to connect with heaven, you will feel its blessings pouring into you.

20 July

Many people are cold and without love, lacking all warmth and light, yet the poor things think that they are going to make a success of their lives! Well no, they must first get used to becoming alive, and the only way to become alive is by learning to love – there are exercises we can do for this too. What exercises? Here is a very easy one. Choose a moment when no one can see you, raise your hand, project all your love towards the earth and sky, to the angels, to the Lord, and say, 'I love you, I love you, I want to be in harmony with you.' In this way, you get into the habit of emanating something vibrant and intense, just like a spring, like the sun.

People always believe that they can hide behind a grim face, expressing neither love nor goodness, not realizing how pernicious this attitude is, as much for themselves as for others. They must learn to express love in order to become alive, so that their face, their gaze – their very presence – emanate life.*

* Related reading: *Harmony and Health,* Izvor No. 225, Chap. 2.

21 July

*A*n idea is a living, active entity. If you do not know this, it is because you are not yet aware of the effects an idea can have upon the depths of your being. Study yourself and you will see how some ideas have harmed you while others, on the contrary, have been a wonderful help to you; then you will understand the importance of nurturing a divine idea, capable of transforming not only your entire being, but everything around you.

The concept of working for the light, for the kingdom of God and his Justice, is the most glorious idea that exists. This idea produces gold within you, meaning that it brings you health, joy, strength, intelligence, hope and faith. Thanks to this idea, you will be regenerated and restored.*

* Related reading: *The High Ideal,* Brochure No. 307.

22 July

*S*omebody goes on holiday, and as they leave they say a little prayer, 'Lord, keep my house safe from thieves!' How amazing – the Lord has to look after their house while they are off travelling and amusing themselves. And if, when they return, they find their house has been burgled, they will be furious with God for failing to do His job. Did they really believe that God would bother guarding their house while they went on holiday? Who do human beings think the Lord is?

So, it is not surprising that from time to time, the spirits on high decide to teach a lesson to heedless folk who think of God as their caretaker: they urge some rascals to rob them. 'But isn't it acceptable to ask God to protect our house?' you will say. Yes, providing you are humble enough to ask Him to send one of His servants, and not to imagine that God Himself will fulfil this role. In addition, you must give something in return for this service by promising to obey divine rules and plans. Humans are extraordinary: they want everything to go their way without giving anything in exchange. No, you must always give something in return for what you have requested.*

* Related reading: *The Faith that Moves Mountains,* Izvor No. 238, Chap. 3.

23 July

Learn to sing together in harmony, with the awareness that you are working on yourselves, of course, but also on the whole world. For the harmony you create gradually spreads outwards and influences every creature in space.

Can you form a whole choir with your individualistic philosophy and your personal quests? No! You are singing a solo. Whereas when there are several of you, you form a choir. It is not enough to work alone and only for oneself. Of course, everyone must work individually, but such work must be done for the good of the collectivity, because the collectivity must be formed of well-developed individuals. So we must do more than seek selfishly to improve ourselves – we must also think to help the collectivity. This new philosophy does not reject the old way of concentrating on individual self-perfection; rather, this self-perfection must always serve the good of the whole. This is what we learn when we sing together in a choir.

24 July

Each day the sun rises, alive and vibrant, sending treasures of light, heat and life throughout space. But there are still some of you who remain insensible to the sunrise, as if there were a screen between you and the sun. And that is so: the life you led the day before, or in the preceding days, has created that screen. Some of you do not realize that your actions, thoughts and feelings might have a harmful or a beneficial influence when you contemplate the rising sun, and that is why the sun means nothing to you.

If you come inwardly prepared to watch the sunrise, you will understand that the sun is a living being, a dazzling world, home to the most highly evolved beings. Thanks to the sun, you can find a solution to all your problems. Yes, because the sun can offer you far more than heat and light: it has the power to open up your mind and your heart.*

* Related reading: *Toward a Solar Civilization,* Izvor No. 201, Chap. 1.

25 July

Nothing can hold out against gratitude. So, every day, keep thanking heaven, until you feel that everything that happens to you is for your good. Begin now by saying, 'Thank you Lord, thank you Lord.' Give thanks for what you have, for what you do not have, for all that gives you happiness, and for all that makes you suffer. In this way, you keep the flame of life alight within you. This is a law that you must know.

You will say, 'But how can we give thanks when we are unhappy, ill or destitute? It just isn't possible.' Yes, it is and that is the greatest secret of all: you must find a reason to be grateful even when you are unhappy. You have no money and are ill? Give thanks and rejoice to see other people rich, healthy and prosperous. Do this and you will see – before long, certain doors will open and blessings will begin to shower down upon you.*

* Related reading: *Golden Rules for Everyday Life,* Izvor No. 227, Chap. 58.

26 July

There are people who think that they can escape trials and suffering by doing away with themselves. In fact, it is even worse afterwards. No one has the right to decide when to die; it is a desertion that will have to be paid for with further suffering. There is no room on high for those who try to enter before their time; they will be turned away and will be obliged to wander in the lower regions of the astral plane for as long as they had left to live on earth.

The attitude of those who commit suicide reveals serious flaws. First, it shows that they are ignorant: they do not understand the reason for the trials they must undergo. Next, they are conceited: they think they know better than heaven what they deserve. Finally, they are weak: they cannot put up with difficulties. So there you have it: ignorance, conceit and weakness. And heaven is displeased because they have abandoned their post. Heaven cannot respect those who put an end to their days, because in doing so, they place themselves above the Lords of all destinies and they will then have to submit to great suffering.

27 July

Decide once and for all to put a stop to all the little sorrows, troubles and annoyances that poison your everyday life. Then you will at last begin to savour peace and freedom.

Observe yourself, and you will see that your life is made difficult not because of great misfortune and calamities, which are not daily occurrences, but because you make mountains from the molehills of a few little irritations or setbacks. This is what can upset or cripple your whole inner life.*

* Related reading: *Love Greater Than Faith,* Izvor No. 239, Chap. 5.

28 July

Go and look at swamps and jungles, and you will see all the animals there devouring each other. Then go much higher up into heavenly regions, among the angelic hierarchies, and you will see nothing but beings who ceaselessly give out love and light. Yes, on high, you will find love and light, whereas down below there is hostility, danger, snares and merciless conflict.

In the same way, people whose occupations and desires have dragged them down to the lower regions are obliged to fight and tear each other to pieces. Then they draw conclusions about life on earth, saying that it is a dog-eat-dog world, where the law of the jungle rules. This is true as long as we stay on a low level. But the higher we climb, the more love and light we find.*

* Related reading: *'Know Thyself' – Jnana Yoga (Part I)*, Complete Works Vol. 17, Chap. III.

29 July

We cannot find something that is exterior to us if we have not first found it within ourselves. Yes, for whatever we come across externally, if we have not already discovered it within, we will pass it by, sight unseen. The more we discover inner beauty, the more we perceive it on the physical plane. No doubt you are thinking, 'If I cannot see it, it is not there.' Yes, it is there, but you do not see it because some of your organs of perception are not yet developed enough.

Strive to seize hold of beauty within, and you will see it outside as well, because the outer, objective world is nothing other than a reflection of the interior, subjective world. So it is pointless to look for something on the outside if you have not first managed to find it within yourself.*

* Related reading: *Golden Rules for Everyday Life,* Izvor No. 227, Chap. 11.

30 July

In order to understand and properly address the problems of social inequality, it is important to know that the conditions in which people find themselves in one incarnation are the result of the way they lived in their previous incarnations.

Workers who are struggling to make a living may revolt and ask, 'Why such injustice?' And their bosses, who find it normal to be well off, and even to live in luxury, do everything they can to retain their privileges. But what neither party knows is that very often, workers who now suffer and complain were once unjust, inhuman bosses, which is why in this incarnation they have been placed in conditions where they must now learn to appreciate the difficulties of former employees. So, bosses must now say to themselves, 'I have the good fortune to enjoy wealth and power in this life, but if I treat my employees unfairly, I shall suffer the consequences in the next life. Lord, help me to make my employees happier.' And there is nothing to prevent employees from praying for their boss to be more enlightened; perhaps they will then reap some benefits.*

* Related reading: *Cosmic Moral Laws,* Complete Works Vol. 12, Chap. IV.

31 July

You seek to develop yourself perfectly in the three worlds – physical, spiritual and divine; you seek love, wisdom and truth; you seek freedom, strength and happiness.

But you must know that your search will be fulfilled only if you have but one aim, one goal in life. Whatever your duties and responsibilities, all your concerns, thoughts, desires, and even the movements of your cells must be directed towards a single end: the kingdom of God and His Justice. When you do this, your energies will be mobilized in such a way that you will be able to achieve all you desire.*

* Related reading: *'In Spirit and in Truth'*, Izvor No. 235, Chap. 5.

1 August

If you wish to win someone's love or friendship, never put pressure on them by means of money, gifts, seduction or blackmail. Even if everyone else uses these methods because they are the easiest, do not use them yourselves.

The only method you have the right to use is light: it is the only truly effective method. Send gifts of spiritual light to those whose love you seek and spread that light all around them. When you want someone to love you, to think of you, send them light: their soul, which will feel the presence of a beneficial entity, will appreciate you more and more.*

* Related reading: *A New Earth – Methods, Exercises, Formulas, Prayers,* Complete Works Vol. 13, Chap. XIV.

2 August

In order to keep the sacred inner fire alight within you, you must feed it pieces of your lower nature every day. Yes, for it is the lower nature, the personality, that is predestined to feed the fire of the spirit. Stop wondering what your lower nature is for and how to get rid of it; without it, not only would survival on earth be impossible, but you would have nothing with which to feed your spirit.

Know that there is a magical law according to which results on the divine plane can be obtained only if you sacrifice something of your personality. And if you go and find an Initiate, a magus or a great Master to ask him to cure you, a member of your family or a friend, for example, or to ensure the success of some enterprise, he will tell you that the only possible way to do so is to renounce certain weaknesses and harmful habits. By abstaining from baser pleasures, we release an energy that fuels our ability to realize all the good we desire, both for ourselves and for others.*

* Related reading: *True Alchemy or the Quest for Perfection,* Izvor No. 221, Chap. 9.

3 August

When children are very small, their only concern is being fed and playing with the things around them, and as soon as they are crossed, they scream and cry. Children are selfish little monsters – yes, but at that age, it is normal and natural. Adults, the father and the mother, understand that they can expect little else. If, however, a child continues to behave in the same way when it grows up, it is scolded or even reprimanded, because it needs to change and stop thinking only of itself. Later on, it will experience the need to be part of a couple and then have children.

Why has Cosmic Intelligence arranged things in this way? To persuade people to look after others besides themselves: a husband or wife and children to start with. But how many people have understood the lesson that Cosmic Intelligence wants to teach them? How many people are able to forget themselves a little, and sincerely think about their wife, their husband and their children in an unselfish way?*

* Related reading: *The Two Trees of Paradise,* Complete Works Vol. 3, Chap. I.

4 August

*S*o many people live any old how the entire day and then in the evening, before going to sleep, they say a little prayer asking God to forgive them their sins. Well, that is not enough. They should know that this behaviour is certain to keep the devil always at their side, like the monk in the following story.

There was once a kindly monk in a monastery who drank and drank. Every day the level of the wine in the barrels went down visibly. He said his prayers every night – somewhat sheepishly of course – and asked God for forgiveness, after which, his mind at rest, he slept peacefully until the following day… when he would start all over again. This went on for years. Then one evening, he forgot to say his prayers, and during the night he felt someone shake him, saying: 'Hey, you didn't say your prayers tonight. Come on, get up, hurry and say your prayers!' He woke up, rubbed his eyes and what did he see? The devil! Yes, it was the devil who had woken him; it was he who urged the monk to say his prayers every night. And why? To stop the monk from mending his ways. Since the monk asked heaven for forgiveness when he said his prayers, his conscience was clear and the next day he would start drinking all over again, to the devil's delight. The story goes that when the monk understood this, he was so frightened that he gave up drinking for good.

5 August

People who meditate on the geometry of crystals and precious stones to understand their structures draw closer to true science – the science of principles. And one day, they will be able to visit the bowels of the earth and see how the spirits of nature work on the minerals. They will visit the sites where billions of intelligent entities work their hardest to reproduce the beauty and perfection of heaven on earth.

In reality, no precious stone, however wonderful it may be, will ever succeed in being an exact reflection of heaven, the beauty of which has no equal. The physical plane is far from being comparable to heaven, but at least it can sometimes give us an image of it. Flowers, precious stones, and so on, are all reflections of the divine world: they remind us, as it were, of the purity, transparency, clarity and perfection of heaven.*

* Related reading: *A New Dawn: Society and Politics in the Light of Initiatic Science (Part II)*, Complete Works Vol. 26, Chap. VI.

6 August

Whatever the psychological and material conditions in which you find yourself, never let yourself be weakened by the thought that evil, in all its forms, could easily befall you. If you always feel weak and vulnerable and without protection, then, yes, you really are exposed.

Work with thought to unite with celestial entities and with light; lead an honest and pure life, and you will be protected. And even if there are people who try to harm you with black magic, it will all fall back on to them, because they will be exposed to the boomerang effect. Evil cannot enter a person who is occupied by the Lord and the angels: it is immediately rejected, and returns to the person who sent it in the first place. Hold on to this idea, and already you will be out of harm's way.

7 August

The masculine attracts the feminine, and the feminine attracts the masculine. Positive attracts negative, and negative attracts positive. That is why all life is subject to the law of alternation – the law of opposites. In the morning, light chases away the darkness of the night, and in the evening, shadows take over again...

Does this mean we can say that night is opposite to day, and day opposite to night? Yes and No. Yes, because light is the opposite of darkness, and no, because day and night work together to create and sustain life. Look around you. Before coming into the world, the child spends nine months hidden inside its mother's womb. For seeds to germinate, they must stay below ground for some time. Bees line their hive with wax combs because they need darkness to make honey, and so on. Any number of tasks begin in the dark before coming out into the light. Light and darkness represent entities, currents and energies that nature uses for its work.*

* Related reading: *Cosmic Creation, Union of the Masculine and Feminine*, Izvor No. 214.

8 August

*D*o you know this tale written by Tolstoy? One day a king picked up a seed that was the size of a hen's egg. He called upon the knowledge of all the sages at his court, but none could tell him where the seed came from. However, he was told of a very old man who lived in his kingdom, who might be able to help. The king sent for the man who arrived supported by two crutches and was nearly blind. The old man examined the seed for a long time and finally said, 'Your Majesty, I do not know what this giant seed is, but if you will allow me, I shall fetch my father who may remember having seen a similar one.' The father arrived, leaning on a single crutch. He was not able to identify the seed either, but he in turn suggested calling upon his own father. The latter soon arrived; he looked like a young man, strong and in good spirits. He took hold of the seed and exclaimed, 'But this is a grain of wheat that used to grow when I was a child. In those days, wheat had very large grains, but since people started to harm each other, steal from each other and massacre each other, the grains of wheat have become smaller and smaller. And if I look so strong and younger than my son and grandson, it is because I continue to live by the rules of honesty and goodness that prevailed during my childhood.'

9 August

If you have people around you who are difficult to bear, it is to teach you to love. One day, when you leave earth and you stand before the celestial entities, they will ask you to account for what you have done on earth. They will say, 'Why did you not love your fellow creatures?'

'Well, because they were nasty, stupid and selfish.'

'No, that is not a reason. Heaven gave you great riches: you received eyes, a mouth, ears, arms and legs, and you were given these to love, not to spread slander, despise, wreak havoc and trample over everyone and everything.'

'But they were so awful!'

'All the more reason to be increasingly generous.'

There are no excuses to justify your behaviour.*

* Related reading: *Golden Rules for Everyday Life,* Izvor No. 227, Chap. 77.

10 August

*T*he heart and the intellect are useful; they are necessary, but they are not enough. In order to gain life's true intelligence, you must develop a third faculty, intuition, which is both an understanding and a feeling. But be careful not to confuse intuition with clairvoyance.

Intuition is superior to clairvoyance. Clairvoyance is a faculty that allows you to see only the objective side of the astral and the mental planes;* you can be clairvoyant and not understand anything you are seeing. Whereas with intuition you may not see anything, but you understand things as if you saw them a hundred times more clearly, because you are experiencing them.**

* See note and diagram on pp. 396 and 397.

** Related reading: *Looking into the Invisible,* Izvor No. 228, Chap. 2.

11 August

It is vital to know how to gauge the measure in all things. Yes, even the measure of goodness, because if you know no bounds, you will inevitably suffer the consequences. Lack of moderation is neither bad nor a crime, but it is a fault, and all faults carry a penalty.

Let me give you an example. A young woman came to see me and said, 'Oh Master, I am so unhappy. I can't stop crying.'

'But why? What has happened?'

'Well, I loved my husband so dearly, I did everything for him, I anticipated all his wishes and always showed him a great deal of affection and warmth, and now he has left me and gone off with one of my friends.'

'Ah, and what is this friend like?'

'Oh, she's selfish and cold.'

'Well, that is just the trouble; you are too warm, he has gone to cool down.'

I can already hear you say, 'So goodness is useless?' Unfortunately, stupid goodness can lead someone into the worst of situations. Even the most marvellous people get hit on the head if they know no bounds. It is not a punishment, no, but through their ignorance, they have set a law in motion, and they receive a few knocks.

12 August

Some call the sun 'the lamp of the universe', to express the idea that the sun illuminates the world and, thanks to its light, we are able to see. And when the sun is not shining on us, we need other sources of light: electric lightbulbs, candles, torches, headlights, and so on. Objects are only visible to the extent that light falls on them and illuminates them: this is a law of the physical world and it is also a law of the spiritual world.

However, there are no lamps in the spiritual world that we can light in the way that we turn on the light in the staircase or in our bedroom. If we want to see, we ourselves have to project light. That is why so few people are able to see on the spiritual plane: because they wait for objects to be illuminated, whereas it is up to them to project the rays of light that will allow them to see.*

* Related reading: *Looking into the Invisible,* Izvor No. 228, Chap. 9.

13 August

ysicists teach us that every particle of matter has an energy. This energy is a masculine principle, and matter is a feminine principle. Our physical body, which consists of matter, also has an energy, and it is this energy that we call the soul. However, human beings are actually made up of several bodies, each of which has a soul.* The physical body has the instinctual soul; the astral body the emotional soul; and the mental body the intellectual soul. And the causal, buddhic and atmic bodies also each have a soul.

Each body has a soul: the body is the vessel and the soul is the content – the two are united. Nature itself, the cosmos, is a body (the body of God), and it has a soul (the universal Soul), which fills the cosmos. All this is crystal-clear. Humans have complicated matters because they lack knowledge, but as far as Initiatic Science is concerned, it is very simple: there are as many souls as there are bodies.

* See note and diagram on pp. 396 and 397.

14 August

*T*he soul needs space: it needs immensity in order to breathe, expand and rejoice. Limit this space and the soul suffocates, wilts and withers away. And that is what happens to people who focus on all the material details of everyday life without ever taking a moment to immerse themselves in immensity and find fulfilment.

Of course, in some cases, limitation is necessary. The birth of a child, for instance, is nothing but a limitation, but it is necessary in order for this manifestation to happen. Human beings who come to incarnate into matter must limit themselves. At the time of death, however, they will return toward immensity. Life is made up of these two processes: limitation and expansion, and to be happy you must know how to apply them both to your daily lives. You enter your innermost being to unite with the universe, with the universal Soul, and then you return to a state of limitation to work. But do not stay in this limited state too long, or you will become bored and will suffer. Think about setting out again soon on the road of immensity.

15 August

The one vital thing that a Master wants to give to his disciples is the light of Initiatic Science, for he knows that once they possess this light, they will be able to face any problem without even needing his presence.

In order to help people, you must give them a spiritual element that becomes part of them. Many people do not realize this. When they want to do good, they give something material instead of remembering that they can give this spiritual element, which will never fade away. They are still unaware of what is essential, so they give money, food and medicines. I am not saying that these are not useful, but if you want to give what is most essential, you must learn to give light.*

* Related reading: *What is a Spiritual Master?*, Izvor No. 207, Chap. 7.

16 August

*T*he need to dominate, to wield power, is so strong in some people that we now see the most materialistic scientists starting to explore the field of Initiatic Science – telepathy, clairvoyance, clairaudience, radiesthesia and psychometry – and they call all this 'parapsychology'. Providing it can give them power over others, they will accept any number of theories they previously considered nonsense. They accept any knowledge of Initiatic Science that can help them achieve their aims, and they reject any knowledge that cannot give them power.

However, using initiatic truths as a means to dominate others is highly immoral, and those who do so will be punished by heaven. You should use this spiritual knowledge only to help and comfort others, to spread light and peace in the world. Then it will be noted in heaven that you are a white magus, and divine blessings will start to rain down upon you.*

* Related reading: *The Living Book of Nature,* Izvor No. 216, Chap. 12.

17 August

*H*ow many times have you heard people say, 'I am so tired!' Yet very few people really know what tiredness is. Tiredness is something that attaches itself to you, the same way some clingy people won't let go of you, always demanding to be loved and kept company. Because people accept tiredness and are preoccupied by it, they reinforce their fatigue so it keeps coming back; it is always there.

So, try to change your attitude and you will see what happens. Let us say that every morning as you wake up you think, 'Oh, I'm so tired, I don't feel like watching the sunrise', and you go back to sleep. Finally, one day you say, 'It's true, I don't feel like getting up, but I want things to change. I'll get up anyway.' So up you get, you wash your face and go out into the fresh air, and suddenly your tiredness has vanished. If you want tiredness to leave you, you must do something about it. If you do nothing to counter it, tiredness will never leave you.

18 August

As long as you do not have a truly spiritual ideal, the forces and energies you carry within you will not be mobilized in the same direction, and the whole of your life will be in disarray.

Look at the life most people lead: what a mess, what chaos! If some people do have an ideal, in the majority of cases it is to get rich, achieve glory and dominate others. In the eyes of heaven, however, that is not an ideal. Of course, these people have a far more original and colourful life than those who content themselves with modest ambitions. You can write novels and make movies about their lives. Yes, and what fascinating stories they make: how they cheated and got the better of a rival, how they ruined a competitor. Perhaps, but sooner or later, heaven will punish them for using their talents to satisfy all their lower tendencies instead of devoting them to the realisation of a divine ideal.*

* Related reading: *The High Ideal,* Brochure No. 307.

19 August

Sometimes you complain, 'I've been watching the sunrise for twenty years and I don't feel any change, no divine seeds are growing within me.' But twenty years is not very long. Some of the seeds buried deep within you need centuries or even millennia, to grow.

In astrology, some planets, like Mercury, Venus and the Moon have a fast revolution and their influence is short and superficial, while others like Jupiter, Saturn, Uranus and Pluto have a slower revolution, which is why their influence is deeper and more tangible.

So, there are some things you can obtain quickly: you can have a job, a house, a spouse and children within a few years. However, learning to be reasonable, patient, in control of oneself or generous takes a very long time, because the 'orbits' of these qualities are vast. That is why you must continue to warm yourself in the rays of the spiritual sun and then, one fine day, everything will grow. Never doubt the effectiveness of the sun in your spiritual life.*

* Related reading: *Toward a Solar Civilization,* Izvor No. 201.

20 August

It is said that the Church and the clergy invented morals in order to dominate and exploit the credulous and ignorant populace. Certainly, in many cases, the clergy used religion in the zealous service of totally shameful purposes.

However, true religion, true morals, are based on a science, the science of cause and consequence, and not on some personal interest. Every thought, every feeling, every action has positive and negative consequences for humans. Where the clergy went wrong was that they did not try to explain the rules they imposed. People were told: 'Do this... do that...' as if they were children who are told to obey, without any explanation. That is why, like children, they disobeyed at the first opportunity. Whereas for their proper evolution, people should have been informed that true religion, like true morality, is based on a knowledge of the great cosmic laws.*

* Related reading: *Looking into the Invisible,* Izvor No. 228, Chap. 10.

21 August

Get into the habit of speaking with love to the flowers, birds, trees, animals and people, for it is a divine habit. Those who know how to say words that warm, invigorate, inspire and kindle the sacred fire, have a magic wand in their mouths.

Always be very attentive to your thoughts and words because, in nature, one of the four elements – earth, water, air or fire – is always there, waiting for the opportunity to clothe everything you think and say in matter. Although this often occurs far away from the person who provided the seeds, it happens unfailingly. Just as the wind sweeps up seeds and sows them far and wide, so your thoughts and words fly away and end up somewhere in space producing results, either good or bad.*

* Related reading: *Golden Rules for Everyday Life,* Izvor No. 227, Chap. 48.

22 August

There are many ways to penetrate the spiritual world. Meditation, together with prayer, is one of the most accessible. Meditation, however, requires preparation. Those who wish to meditate without having first acquired an internal discipline – that is, control over their thoughts, feelings and desires – will begin by wandering in the lower regions of the astral plane,* stirring up layers of darkness inhabited by entities that are often hostile to human beings. That is how they fall prey to hallucinations bearing no relation to the object of their meditation.

So before meditating, you should start by putting your psychic being in order, otherwise even an exercise as useful and beneficial as meditation can become dangerous.**

* See note and diagram on pp. 396 and 397.

** Related reading: *Meditation,* Brochure No. 302.

23 August

*P*hysically, a person can only be a man or a woman, and it is generally impossible to be mistaken on this point. Psychically, however, things are far more complex. Psychically, every human being has the two principles: the masculine and the feminine. Man can therefore not be likened to the masculine principle, nor woman to the feminine principle. In the Chinese representation of yin and yang, for instance, the black, feminine yin contains a white dot, and the white, masculine yang contains a black dot, to explain that the masculine always contains a feminine part, and vice versa.

Living men and women are not abstract principles: living men and women are a combination of masculine and feminine in unequal proportions and, what is more, from one incarnation to another they may even change sex physically. For it has been established by Cosmic Intelligence that, in order to grow and perfect themselves, people should know the two states, the two conditions, and so learn to acquire the qualities of both principles fully.*

* Related reading: *Cosmic Balance, The Secret of Polarity*, Izvor No. 237, Chap. 15.

24 August

*E*ven if you are not aware of it, everything around you influences you. The important thing is to become aware of precisely this fact so you can work constructively on yourself. As soon as you sense that a creature, an object or a natural phenomenon has a positive effect on you, make a conscious effort to open your inner doors to allow these influences to penetrate deep within you. If you do not open yourself up, even the best things will remain ineffective; they will not touch you.

Go to a gushing spring or fountain and imagine that it is gushing and flowing within you. Go to the sun, contemplate it, open yourself up to it, so that it may awaken all the warmth and light of your inner spiritual sun. Go to the flowers and ask them the secret of their colour and their scent, and listen to them so that you, too, may learn to extract the most fragrant quintessence from your heart and soul.*

* Related reading: *Golden Rules for Everyday Life,* Izvor No. 227, Chap. 104.

25 August

When a society makes its economic interests its prime concern, even if this society initially achieves success, the day will inevitably come when it is confronted with problems that it did not have the wisdom to foresee.

Here is an example: there is nothing more profitable for a country that manufactures arms than to export those arms. That is how an assortment of increasingly lethal weapons is sold to peoples who risk jeopardizing the peace and safety of the entire planet with their endless fighting. Some of these peoples can barely read and write, but that does not stop arms dealers from supplying them with the most sophisticated weapons, even sending experts to train them in their use. On the one hand, a great deal of money is made – that is true. But on the other, these profits will have to be paid for dearly because afterwards, how expensive and difficult it is to put a stop to the conflicts breaking out all over the world! In the end, we face insurmountable problems because we did not think things through, we were not far-sighted –we considered only the immediate benefits.*

* Related reading: *Under the Dove, the Reign of Peace,* Izvor No. 208, Chap. 7.

26 August

Creation is the work of the number 2. But what is this number 2? It is the number 1 polarized into positive and negative, masculine and feminine, active and passive. As soon as there is manifestation, there is partition, division. In order for number 1 to manifest and make itself known, it must divide. Unity is the privilege of God Himself, His exclusive domain. In order to create, God – the 1 – had to become 2: in 1 there can be no creation because no exchanges are possible. God therefore projected Himself out of Himself by polarizing, and the universe was born from the existence of these two poles. The positive pole attracts the negative pole and the negative pole attracts the positive. This mechanism of reciprocal action and reaction sparks off and maintains the movement of life. Stopping this movement would lead to stagnation and death, the return to the initial state of non-differentiation.

The first lines of the *Book of Genesis* tell how creation occurred through a succession of divisions. On the first day of creation, God separated light from darkness. On the second day, He separated the waters above from the waters below. On the third day, He gathered the waters from dry land. 1 is therefore an entity enclosed within itself. In order to be released, this entity must become 2.

27 August

We must work according to the laws of wisdom and the methods of love. Love and wisdom can be compared to the hands of a clock: wisdom is the small hand that marks the hours, and love is the big hand that marks the minutes. Wisdom shows us the high ideal, the programme to be realized, and this programme is valid throughout eternity. But in order to realize this programme, we must adopt the methods of love, that is, live every minute of the day with joy and enthusiasm, without ever losing our impetus. That is the way to reconcile the programme of eternity with that of the day. Wisdom shows the direction in which to travel, and love – the heart – maintains the movement.*

* Related reading: *'Walk While You Have the Light'*, Izvor No. 244, Chap. 3.

28 August

A child who is always good and obedient will be considered 'sweet and adorable' by adults. Of course, it is easier to cope with a child who sits still when told not to move, who keeps silent when told to be quiet, and so on, but what will become of this sweet, docile child later in life? Not a great deal: this child will remain unremarkable.

Whereas a wilful and unruly child causes trouble for those around him. His parents, neighbours and educators endlessly complain, 'Oh, he has gone too far, look what he has done now!' Yes, but the child whom everyone finds tiresome and a nuisance is far more likely to become somebody. At the moment, this child is said to overstep the limits, but once he has learned to channel his energies, he will stand out because of his character and talent. And the parents and educators, whose task it is to ensure that he flourishes, must help the child to do so.*

* Related reading: *Cosmic Balance, The Secret of Polarity*, Izvor No. 237, Chap. 2.

29 August

*O*nly through purity can we develop intuition. That is why, in our teaching, we attach such great importance to purity: living a pure life, eating pure food, drinking pure drink, breathing pure air, having pure thoughts and pure feelings.

A person's whole destiny depends on the clarity of their 'inner eye', and this clarity depends on their way of life. As soon as they make a mistake and violate divine laws, their spiritual vision clouds over, so they are no longer forewarned or guided, and they become entrenched in inextricable complications. So, try to become aware at last of the relationship that exists between your day-to-day behaviour and the clarity of your vision. Those who decide to live an upright, honest and noble life purify themselves, and their subtle organs start to function. That is how, with proper guidance and direction, they will again find the springs, fields, lakes, meadows and mountains of their true homeland.*

* Related reading: *The Mysteries of Yesod,* Complete Works Vol. 7, Chap. I.

30 August

Nature is alive and intelligent. Yes, intelligent. Intelligence is not unique to human beings. Of course, some people find this very difficult to accept, but they must realize that as our opinion of nature changes, so we alter our destiny.

Nature is the body of God. If we think it is dead and stupid, we diminish the life within us; and if we think that nature is alive and intelligent, that stones, plants, animals and stars are alive and intelligent, we also introduce life into ourselves. And since nature is alive and intelligent, we must be extremely attentive and respectful towards it, and look upon it with a sense of sacredness.*

* Related reading: *The Fruits of the Tree of Life – The Cabbalistic Tradition,* Complete Works Vol. 32, Chap. XXII.

31 August

What is the respective place of men and women? The day will come when men and women will have to sort out this problem, for it keeps pitting them against one another. For centuries, even millennia, men have imposed their dominance on women, and now we are beginning to see a reversal of the situation: women are standing up for themselves. They no longer accept being submissive to men; they want equal rights and are even prepared to play the masculine role, usurping men's position.

This is normal; it is the law of compensation. Men have gone too far. Instead of being paragons of honesty, goodness and righteousness in order to earn women's admiration and esteem, men have abused their authority and physical superiority over women. They have given themselves all the rights, and imposed only obligations on women. How could men ever think that this situation could last?*

* Related reading: *Cosmic Balance, The Secret of Polarity,* Izvor No. 237, Chap. 4.

1 September

In the beginning, God, the primordial Fire, the masculine principle, engendered light and projected it into space. Light is the substance of creation. This is why the *Book of Genesis* says that God created light from the beginning, on the first day.

Some theologians and philosophers claim that God created the world out of nothing. Out of nothing external, yes, and this is what is difficult to understand, for we human beings always need external materials and tools to build something. The truth is that it is impossible to create something out of nothing. This notion of a creation that came from nothing simply means that God drew the substance of the universe from his own being. The universe is the very substance drawn from God, which now exists externally in the form of light… but which is still God.*

* Related reading: *Truth, Fruit of Wisdom and Love,* Izvor No. 234, Chap. 12.

2 September

*M*ost people readily admit that they need instruction when it comes to the practical, intellectual or artistic aspects of life, but they dismiss the idea that they have something to learn about how to conduct their inner life. This is a very dangerous attitude, for those who reject the experience and teaching of the spiritual masters cut themselves off from these living 'books' who could teach them the essential things they need to know. They should not be surprised if they eventually find themselves in a tight spot, and fate deals them a few blows.

It is very important to have a Master or to be in touch with the luminous spirits of the invisible world. When we link ourselves to these beings, whose experience is so much greater than ours, who have already solved so many problems, their knowledge becomes available to us and we can draw on it as the need arises. We live, we act, and something else comes and adds itself to our own experience, something higher and richer that helps us.*

* Related reading: *Love and Sexuality (Part II),* Complete Works Vol. 15, Chap. VI.

3 September

Because of your selfish, malicious, vindictive thoughts and feelings, your astral and mental bodies* have become so opaque that you can no longer communicate with the realities and beings of the spiritual world. You want to meditate, but as you are unable to rid yourself of your prosaic cares and worries, of your resentment and irritation, of the weight of old memories, you cannot elevate yourselves.

However long you sit still with your eyes closed, waiting for that movement that will enable your soul to leap up to the light, nothing happens. In such circumstances, it is virtually pointless to try and meditate, for you will achieve nothing. Your inner instruments cannot function because they are clogged. And this will be the case until you have understood that the most important work in life is to strip away all that encumbers your inner life. Of course, this is difficult, but you will never get anywhere until you have at least begun this work.**

* See note and diagram on pp. 396 and 397.

** Related reading: 'In Spirit and in Truth', Izvor No. 235, Chap. 7.

4 September

Morality and religion preach that we should forget ourselves and think only of others. This is wonderful, but is it really possible? Ask the sun what it thinks. 'O sun, you who give light and warmth and life to all creatures, do you really think only of them?' And the sun will reply, 'No, of course not! I think only of myself. If I pour out my blessings on all creatures, it is because I want to. That is what I enjoy doing. And this is why I do not wonder endlessly if they deserve all these gifts. I don't care one way or the other. I leave them free and in peace, and continue to illuminate and warm them, because it gives me pleasure to do so.'

So you see, even the sun agrees that the need to think of oneself never disappears, it just takes on different forms, depending on the degree of evolution of the beings concerned. We must take care of others, yes, but for our own satisfaction, for our own development. It is impossible to forget oneself, to renounce oneself entirely. What we should do is think of ourselves in a new way, until that way becomes as altruistic and as generous as that of the sun.

5 September

*H*uman beings are instinctively driven to climb the social ladder and, in order to do so, they must pass certain exams or win a competition. They have this desire because they know that if they are in a higher position they will be better paid while working less and, above all, they will have greater opportunities to act, to manage things and take charge of the situation.* But why have they never realized that it is exactly the same in the spiritual realm?

Initiates and true disciples know that on the spiritual plane there are other committees and examiners who test them, weigh them up and give out diplomas. So, instead of competing with human beings for the position of governor, minister or president, they focus all their efforts on the inner, spiritual, divine plane. The nearer they come to the summit, to perfection, the higher the rank and the greater the powers accorded them by heaven… until one day, they are even able to command the very forces of nature.

* Related reading: *A New Dawn: Society and Politics in the Light of Initiatic Science (Part I),* Complete Works Vol. 25, Chap. IV.

6 September

*S*o many everyday actions have a symbolic significance of which people are totally ignorant. Have you ever thought about the meaning of sewing or embroidery? If you succeed in deciphering what the cloth, the needle, the thread and the design represent, you will understand that embroidery tells the whole story of life.

The cloth is the feminine principle, the matter upon which the needle works. The needle is the will, the masculine principle that guides the thread, that is to say, thought. A needle can be threaded with strands that may be valuable or ordinary, colourful or drab, sturdy or fragile, and it can produce a design on the cloth that may be magnificent or very plain. The cloth can also represent the physical body. Through the impulse of the will, your thoughts work at the embroidery, and the design that begins to take shape is seen in the form of your body, the lines of your face, the expression of your eyes, which all tell the story of your life. Those who understand what it means to sew and embroider will become Initiates – that is, true artists. For only Initiates know how each one of us must work on the raw material of our own being in order to give it the most harmonious and radiant form.

7 September

Many forms of illness are simply an accumulation of foreign elements that the body has been unable to eliminate. In order to be cured you have to get rid of them. Cleansing, therefore, is one of the most effective ways of keeping healthy.

But there is something even more important than cleansing, and that is vigilance in choosing which elements to absorb. The reason it is so important to harvest the particles the sun brings us every morning is that they are the only ones that produce no wastes, no impurities in our organism. Everything we eat, drink and breathe always leaves some waste. Of course, this must not stop us from eating, drinking and breathing. But at the same time we must learn to nourish ourselves with a far superior element – sunlight.*

* Related reading: *Life and Work in an Initiatic School – Training for the Divine,* Complete Works Vol. 30, Chap. VII.

8 September

If you look closely at the symbolism contained in the image of the sun, you will have to acknowledge that it is the best representation of God we could have. And we clearly have a great deal of inner work to do with this image of the sun. You can look at the sun for years and imagine all kinds of things about it, but until you feel it vibrating, radiating, pulsating within you, it will be foreign to you. It will have nothing to say to you. It would even be pointless to go and look at it. You will be warmed and invigorated a little, and you will receive a few calories and 'vitamins', but you will not discover that which is essential.

What is essential is to find your inner sun, which is the sign that the Deity dwells within you. At that point, you will no longer even need books or pictures, temples, statues or crosses… not even the physical sun or the stars. You will draw everything you need from within, from your inner sun.*

* Related reading: *'In Spirit and in Truth',* Izvor No. 235, Chap. 15.

9 September

*T*he spirit descends towards matter and matter rises towards the spirit. This is why human beings, who through their links to the physical plane represent matter, must reach up towards the spirit, their own spirit, God.

A river flowing down from the heights has the right to split up into smaller tributaries in order to water the land through which it flows. The sun too has the right to distribute its rays throughout space in order to bring life to the whole solar system. But we, who are on the periphery, must not scatter or disperse ourselves. On the contrary, we must strive with all our being towards the centre, the summit, so as to receive life and strength from it. One day, perhaps, we too shall have the right to disperse ourselves like the sun, but only once we have succeeded in identifying ourselves with the centre, when we have become as powerful, radiant and vital as the sun. Then, yes, like the sun, we will be able to project our love and light on all creatures.*

* Related reading: *Know Thyself' – Jnana Yoga (Part I)*, Complete Works Vol. 17, Chap. III.

10 September

It is not a question of belonging to one religion rather than another, of observing one rite rather than another. A rite is only a form, and forms are useful only to the extent to which we are capable of bringing life to them, of giving them content.

To take Communion with the host and wine, for example, is an empty gesture unless we have learned to communicate with the Creator in a much broader, deeper way in all the simplest acts of everyday life: eating and drinking, walking, breathing, looking and listening, sleeping, loving and working. Yes, while we are breathing, while we are sleeping or gazing at the beauties of nature, at the mountains, oceans, sun or the stars, we can also experience magnificent states of consciousness that are communion. This is the only true communion, which gives meaning to the Christian rite of Communion.*

* Related reading: *The Yoga of Nutrition,* Izvor No. 204, Chap. 8.

11 September

Never forget that it is your work with thought that is the most important for your future. It is this work that will enable you, day by day, to move closer to the fulfilment of your ideal. Every day, by means of your prayers and meditation, you add an element to the edifice – a brick, a block, some mortar, a plank, a nail, and so on.

What a joy it is to feel that you are doing something, that you are making progress! It may well be that your joy will be less when you finally complete your edifice; yes, you may feel a little let down when it is already done. Human beings find more happiness in work, activity and hope, and in the thought that there is always something more to discover and to achieve, than in the accomplishment.*

* Related reading: *Cosmic Moral Laws,* Complete Works Vol. 12, Chap. XI.

12 September

Learn to listen to what the sages of the East call the 'voice of silence' speaking within you. Silence, true silence, has a voice, for it is not a void, it is not death. On the contrary, it is the expression of fulfilment and true life.

The voice of silence is the voice of God. We can hear it speaking within us only when we have managed to quell all our inner agitation, all our inner revolt, fear and greed, because we then allow our higher nature, and our higher nature alone, to express itself.*

* Related reading: *The Path of Silence,* Izvor No. 229, Chap. 12.

13 September

A school of young fish were listening to their teacher explaining the pitfalls of life, particularly the danger of hooks. While all the other students were taking notes and drawing pictures of a hook so that they would recognize one when they saw it, at the back of the class was one little fish who, finding the lesson terribly boring, slipped out of school and wandered off on his own. As he was swimming about, he saw a worm wriggling in the water, and as he was starting to feel hungry, he dashed at it and swallowed it in one gulp. Oh, but what was that stabbing pain in his throat? He wriggled and fought so hard that he managed to free himself, but what a sorry state he was in! He went back to school and shamefacedly told the teacher what had happened. 'Now I understand that you know more about life than I do. You wanted to warn me about certain dangers, but I didn't want to listen to you, and I was hooked.'

Ah yes, this is a story for children, but there are a great many adults who are no wiser than that little fish. They want to be free to live in their own way, and they think they can get by without any lessons from the wise. With such a mentality they too are in danger of being hooked – but will they be as lucky as this little fish and manage to escape?

14 September

The spiritual world is superior to the physical world because not being material it is safe from outside attacks. Nobody can take hold of thoughts, feelings or beliefs. Even if you are deprived of your books or your laboratory, or locked up in prison, no one can prevent you from feeling rich and free, and from continuing to reflect and carry on experiments in your inner laboratories. This is why it is so important to learn to reinforce and enrich your inner world. It is the only way to have something that really and truly belongs to you.*

* Related reading: *Golden Rules for Everyday Life,* Izvor No. 227, Chap. 10.

15 September

*T*he reason why human beings fail to evolve is that they neglect certain truths, truths that they should remind themselves of ten, twenty, thirty times a day. Yes, when you get carried away and do things that are not very fair or noble – that you later regret – you must tell yourself that it was because you had forgotten the truths and laws that would have allowed you to triumph over your weaknesses.

You must recognize how useful repetition is.* Besides, there are so many things that you find normal to repeat. Every day you are willing to eat and drink several times, to sleep, to breathe… or to make the same foolish mistakes. But you cannot bear to hear someone repeating truths that can save you. Is that intelligent?

* Related reading: *Life and Work in an Initiatic School – Training for the Divine,* Complete Works Vol. 30, Chap. VIII.

16 September

All those who have family, social, professional or political responsibilities must strive to reach the highest viewpoint within themselves from which they can control all aspects of the problems they have to resolve. In this way, their decisions will be the fairest for everyone involved. You will say, 'Even if their decisions are fair, they may not be accepted. Most people care only about defending their own selfish interests. It is not easy to get them to consider other people's welfare.' That is true, but even if some people reject your sound analysis and conclusions, that is no reason to abandon your efforts. Once you succeed in raising yourself up to this higher viewpoint, there will be other opportunities in life to make it prevail.

No effort to advance on the path of lucidity and altruism is ever wasted. You must not be discouraged, even if others brand you as a dreamer, a utopian, a visionary or a crank – there is no shortage of labels – for you know that you are getting closer to the truth.*

* Related reading: *'In Spirit and in Truth'*, Izvor No. 235, Chap. 6.

17 September

*I*nitiates do not reject the physical world. They rejoice and marvel at everything, and make use of everything, but they do not delude themselves: they never confuse the ends with the means. They know that what is essential is within human beings themselves, and that the outer world must be at the service of the inner world.* For light is within us; truth and peace are within us; the kingdom of God is within us. It is within ourselves that we must seek these things. All external things are simply the husks, the shadow of reality. In certain circumstances they can be useful and effective, but they are not absolutely real; they are just images that can crumble and disappear. And those who cling to them find not the spirit but matter, not truth but illusion.

In every realm of life, you must always try to look further than the form, otherwise your spiritual needs will never be satisfied, and you will be unhappy. Whereas if you are accustomed to seeing the infinite affinities between each form and the divine world, you will go a long way. You must learn to read the book that is lying open before you.

* Related reading: *The Powers of Thought,* Izvor No. 224, Chap. 9.

18 September

All human beings were created in the Lord's workshops according to the same blueprint, with the same elements, and they therefore have the same structure, they are driven by the same forces. In descending into matter, however, they followed different paths and had different experiences, which awakened in them different and even conflicting opinions, tendencies and tastes. And as everyone is convinced that their particular view of truth represents the only truth, they are incapable of understanding each other, and discord and conflict are the order of the day in every domain.

If they are to restore unity, to understand and appreciate the same values, human beings must set out inwardly once again on the ascending path that leads to the summit, to the luminous realms of the spirit. Yes, if, instead of remaining down below and continuing their endless arguments, they would just make up their minds to adopt the viewpoint of the summit, all their political, economic, social and religious problems could be solved in twenty-four hours. For there is one thing you should get into your heads: to truly resolve a problem, you must not remain on the same level as the issue, but do inner work so as to look at it from a higher viewpoint.

19 September

*T*ell yourself that there will always be people who criticize you or try to dampen your enthusiasm because they do not know what is in your heart and soul. Instead of becoming discouraged and abandoning your work, or wanting to seek revenge, you must redouble your efforts. Remind yourself that you have all the resources you need, that heaven has given you all kinds of possibilities, faculties and energies, and that it is up to you to hold fast and continue your work. Why give up your evolution and your inner enrichment because of the judgment and ill will of others? Are they so important that you should bow to their opinion? Keep up the good work, and one day they will be forced to recognize that they were mistaken about you.*

* Related reading: *Youth: Creators of the Future,* Izvor No. 233, Chap. 15.

20 September

Some people think that the mere fact they possess and venerate something that once belonged to a saint makes them spiritual. Not at all! People can call themselves spiritualists and still behave like complete materialists.

Whether you are a materialist or a spiritual person depends on your level of consciousness. Interest in the invisible world does not make you spiritual, nor does interest in matter make you a materialist. It all depends on how you are interested in the spirit or in matter. The way some people practise religion is, in fact, no more than materialism. This is why, instead of criticizing materialists, many people would do better to look at themselves, and ask themselves if they are not also materialists, since they focus exclusively on the form, losing sight of both content and meaning. Do you want to be a genuinely spiritual person? Then seek the spirit that gives life and the truth that makes you free.*

* Related reading: 'In Spirit and in Truth', Izvor No. 235, Chap. 12.

21 September

*T*he best way of getting through life's trials is to put yourself in the service of the Lord and work for the coming of His kingdom.

When you work selflessly for the good of humanity, you enter into the abundance of the great Universal White Brotherhood on high. All your brothers and sisters in the divine world each begin to take on a part of your burdens – they help you to bear your suffering. Yes, but you must understand that this is a phenomenon that takes place in our consciousness. You will not be helped on the physical, material plane, but on the psychic and spiritual planes. So, work for the coming of the kingdom of God. If you work only for yourself, you will have to endure your destiny.*

* Related reading: *Truth, Fruit of Wisdom and Love,* Izvor No. 234, Chap. 18.

22 September

*A*rchangel Michael presides over the autumn equinox, which occurs on September 22. The sun enters Libra, ushering in a new season. Fruits fall from the trees, leaving their empty husks on the ground; seeds are sorted and consumed, or stored and sown later so that a new cycle can begin.

But nature's work of separating and sorting does not apply only to vegetation; it also concerns the destiny of human beings. Just as the fruit is separated from the tree, and the seed from the fruit, so is the soul one day separated from the body. The body is the envelope of the soul, and the soul is the seed that is planted on high in heaven. When the fruit of a human being is ripe, it must not fall to the ground like the seed of a plant; it must soar up to heaven.*

* Related reading: *The Fruits of the Tree of Life – The Cabbalistic Tradition,* Complete Works Vol. 32, Chap. XVII.

23 September

*T*he path of initiation is very long and very difficult, make no mistake about it. Those who claim that it is possible to become a clairvoyant, a magus or an Initiate in three months or a year are deluding themselves and deluding others as well. No sooner have they learned about certain spiritual practices than many people believe they are Masters, already qualified to instruct others. Well, No. That is impossible.

You must study and practise for a very long time before you are able to guide others in the spiritual life, otherwise you will be courting disaster both for yourself and for them. Of course, even if you are not very advanced, you can always teach what you already know. But you must never teach what you do not know and what you are still incapable of realizing. As we have often seen, when the blind try to lead the blind, they fall off the cliff together!*

* Related reading: *The Seeds of Happiness,* Izvor No. 231, Chap. 2.

24 September

When an Initiate opens his door in the morning, he raises his hand in greeting to the whole of nature, to the sky and the sun. He says good morning to the new day and all creation. By this gesture he establishes communication with the source of life, and nature responds to this greeting. He also greets the angels of the four elements: the angels of air, earth, water and fire, as well as the gnomes, undines, sylphs and salamanders – who then sing and dance for joy! He says 'Hello! Hello! Good morning!' to the trees and stones and even to the wind.

Try this for yourselves. You will feel that something within you finds its balance, becomes more harmonious, and much that is obscure and bewildering will fade away simply because you have decided to greet living nature and all the creatures that inhabit it.*

* Related reading: *A New Earth – Methods, Exercises, Formulas, Prayers,* Complete Works Vol. 13, Chap. VIII.

25 September

A spiritual Master is a being who has achieved total control of his thoughts, feelings and actions. Perhaps you think that that is no great achievement. In fact, it is everything. Mastery of all one's thoughts, feelings and actions presupposes a discipline and special methods based on very profound knowledge. This knowledge concerns the structure of human beings, the forces at work within them, and the correspondences between their whole being (that is, both their physical and their subtle bodies) and the different planes of the visible and invisible worlds. To be master of oneself also means that one knows the entities of the invisible world and the structure of the universe as a whole.

A spiritual Master is a being who has resolved the essential problems of life. He is free, his will is strong, and above all, he is filled with love, kindness, gentleness and light.*

* Related reading: *The Second Birth,* Complete Works Vol. 1, Chap. VII.

26 September

We think we know nature but actually, we do not know it. All that we see around us – forests, mountains, rivers and seas – is no more than the outer wrappings, different layers of physical matter; its clothes, if you wish. You must endeavour to look beyond that in order to see and sense the vibrations and emanations of the etheric body* of nature. In fact, even the etheric body is a garment. We have to look even further.

Only those who are able to divest nature of all its garments can know truth. This is what the disciples were taught in the ancient initiations: to draw aside the veil of Isis.** In the religion of Egypt, the goddess Isis was the wife of the god Osiris. She was the great feminine figure in whom the Initiates saw a symbol of primordial Nature, from which came forth all the beings and all the elements of creation. This Nature, impenetrable to ordinary men and women, is the Initiates' principal object of study. They want to know it, which is why they strive to understand all the forms of existence to which it has given rise and through which it manifests itself.

* See note on p. 396.
** Related reading: 'In Spirit and in Truth', Izvor No. 235, Chap. 7.

27 September

It can be said that there are three categories of beings, and that each category is governed by its own law.

Primitive beings, who in repeated incarnations have sought to satisfy only their coarsest needs, are subject to the law of necessity. They are so firmly entrenched in matter that they have no freedom of movement; for them there is but one path, a very hard one that they are obliged to follow.

The law of free will governs those who are more highly evolved, those whose thoughts and actions in previous incarnations give them a certain freedom of choice today. Their freedom has its limits, of course, but they can choose between at least two possibilities. This category includes the disciples of all spiritual teachings, and all those who seek to make progress.

As for the law of divine providence, this is the law that governs the great Masters and great Initiates. Life lies open before them, vast and splendid. They are truly free, for light dwells within them.*

* Related reading: *Truth, Fruit of Wisdom and Love,* Izvor No. 234, Chap. 18.

28 September

Angels govern the four elements – earth, water, air and fire – and these angels are God's servants. That is why we can ask the Lord to send his angels to help us in our spiritual work.

Here is a prayer you can say: 'Lord God almighty, Creator of heaven and earth, Master of the universe, I beg you to send me your servants, the four angels. The Angel of Earth, that he may absorb all the wastes of my physical body so that it becomes able to express your splendour, and that your will may be manifested through it. The Angel of Water, that he may wash all impurities from my heart, and fill it with selfless love. The Angel of Air, that he may purify my intellect so that wisdom and light might settle in it. Finally, Lord, send me the Angel of Fire, that he may sanctify my soul and my spirit, so that your truth may dwell in them, and so that I may work for your kingdom and your righteousness. Amen. Amen. Amen. So may it be!'*

---

* Related reading: *The Fruits of the Tree of Life – The Cabbalistic Tradition,* Complete Works Vol. 32, Chap. VII.

29 September

*T*he principal role in the purification of the earth belongs to Archangel Michael. During the course of the centuries, multitudes of evil beings have spewed destructive forces into the universe, which have accumulated and taken the form of a monster known as the Dragon or Serpent. Daring, selfless men and women have waged a relentless fight against the Dragon but to this day, none has succeeded in vanquishing it. Archangel Michael is the only one capable of defeating this egregor. Together with his army, he will accomplish what the multitudes have been asking of the Creator for centuries. His intervention has been foretold in *Revelation* and other books of sacred scripture.

This is why we should link ourselves to Archangel Michael and ask him to protect us and allow us to unite our efforts to his in order to strengthen his victory. The children of God listed among those who take part in the combat led by Archangel Michael, this solar spirit, this most luminous power of God, will receive the kiss of the Angel of Fire. And this kiss, will not burn them, it will illuminate them.*

---

* Related reading: *The Fruits of the Tree of Life – The Cabbalistic Tradition,* Complete Works Vol. 32, Chap. XVII.

30 September

The most important thing for the conduct of our life is to know that everything is one. Of course, to all appearances, the philosophy of duality seems closer to the truth, given how the world endlessly presents a sorry spectacle of battles, conflicts, clashes and rivalries of every kind.

Human beings are pitted against each other, but in reality, they are one. If they separate it spells death for all, and this is precisely what they fail to see. So while they fight one another and appear to be separate, they are linked, they are sustained by unity. On this Cosmic Tree of unity, there are many branches, leaves and fruits that frequently jostle each other, but this cannot alter the fact that they all stem from the same trunk and the same roots, on which they depend for their very survival.*

* Related reading: *'In Spirit and in Truth'*, Izvor No. 235, Chap. 5, Part 2.

1 October

There may be moments when you feel that you are suddenly filled with light: from one instant to the next your consciousness soars up to the plane of the superconscious, and you are dazzled by this immensity, this beauty.

Unfortunately, this does not last, and you soon return to your everyday life, with the same worries and the same weaknesses. You feel as though you were an isolated fragment in the dark, cut off from the whole, from the Divine, from your own higher Self. Then, sometime later, everything is clear and bright again – but this too does not last. Do not let this discourage you. One day, after all these ups and downs,* the light will no longer leave you; you will have crossed to the other shore and you will be saved for good.

* Related reading: *The Faith that Moves Mountains,* Izvor No. 238, Chap. 6 and Chap. 10.

2 October

*A*dults have still not fully understood how they should behave with children and, in particular, they are careless about the way in which they speak to them. So many parents and educators keep telling them that they are useless, dunces or idiots, and the children, influenced by suggestion, as if hypnotized, actually do become stupid and useless after a while.

It is important to know that the spoken word is powerful, active and that what adults say to children can have a very harmful influence on them, can inhibit them and frighten them. Are threats about the big bad wolf, the police, the devil or who knows what else really necessary in order to get them to be good and obedient? These children are likely to feel threatened and in danger for the rest of their lives and will become neurotic. There are many things adults need to correct about their attitude towards children; otherwise, what they call an upbringing will in fact be a knocking down.

3 October

*T*he principles that govern the universe are like the numbers from zero to nine, from which stem all numerical combinations. Principles,* like the first ten numbers, are immutable, but it is beyond us to predict the myriad combinations they can produce – these permutations are infinite.

This is what we must learn: the new combinations and new forms engendered over the course of centuries by the principles, which themselves are eternal. Movement is the law of life that applies in every realm. This is why religions are making such a great mistake when they try and make forms last forever. Only principles are eternal; forms must change.

* Related reading: *'In Spirit and in Truth'*, Izvor No. 235, Chap. 11.

4 October

If human beings are always dissatisfied and disappointed, it is because they rely too heavily on material things to make them happy – a new house or car, a better-paid job, a post as minister or president, and so on. To begin with, of course, they are delighted. Who wouldn't be? But after a while, they are forced to recognize that they are not so happy anymore, they need something more. Unfortunately, such things as cars, houses and money do not grow on trees, so they will continue to feel dissatisfied until the day they understand that true joy* and happiness do not come from material possessions, but from possessions of the soul and spirit.

And spiritual possessions are, of course, very different from material possessions. For example, you can go for a walk and rejoice in the beauty of nature, of the sun, stars and mountains. You do not actually possess them, but they inspire feelings, thoughts and emotions. These are the true possessions that will never disappoint you: the events of your inner life, what goes on in your heart and soul.

* Related reading: *The Wellsprings of Eternal Joy,* Izvor No. 242, Chaps. 9, 13 and 17.

5 October

There are days when your voice is warm, full, expressive and vivifying, and other days when it is flat, lifeless, husky or grating. If your voice changes in this way, it is because it is influenced by your state of mind. This is why you should always try to live in a state of inner harmony, for this will influence your vocal cords.

The higher your level of consciousness, the clearer and more crystalline, vibrant and powerful the sounds you produce, and the more beneficial their influence on other creatures. When you learn to put your voice* in the service of the forces of light, you will be contributing to dispelling the darkness weighing on the world. The children of God should know these great laws so as to do good.

* Related reading: *Creation: Artistic and Spiritual,* Izvor No. 223, Chap. 5.

6 October

Fire and water* are expressions of the two principles, masculine and feminine, that work together in the universe. When a man and woman unite, they reproduce the union of fire and water, and if they do not know how to go about it, water – the woman – will evaporate, and fire – the man – will be extinguished. As fire and water can destroy each other, they are said to be enemies. On the face of it, it is true that men and women are perpetually in conflict, and yet, for some reason, they continue to seek each other out. What is that reason? It is that they represent the two great cosmic principles that together create life.

However, if fire and water are truly to create life instead of destroying each other, they must not be in direct contact. The water must be poured into a container and placed over the fire. In this way, the fire will exalt the water, generating a substantial release of energy by means of which the two will set the whole world in motion.

* Related reading: *The Mysteries of Fire and Water,* Izvor No. 232.

7 October

If you meditate on the phrase from *Genesis,* *'God said, Let there be light,'* together with the opening words of *St John's Gospel, 'In the beginning was the Word, and the Word was with God, and the Word was God',* you will discover that light is the substance that the divine Word, the firstborn of God, brought forth to serve as the matter of creation.

You will say that when you look at stones, plants, animals or even human beings, you cannot see that they are made of light. Yes, but that is because the light of which they are made has been condensed to such a degree that it has become opaque. And if light and matter are generally seen as opposites, it is because we do not know that what we call matter is actually condensed light.*

* Related reading: *The Yoga of Nutrition,* Izvor No. 204, Chaps. 3 and 5.

8 October

*T*he Kabbalah* says that the serpent is allowed to rise only as far as certain sephiroth, and that it can never reach the highest region formed by *Kether, Chokmah* and *Binah*.** And since we are created in the image of the universe, there is a region within us, too, where evil no longer finds the conditions it needs to exist.

The light and the intensity of vibrations that prevail in the higher regions of our being and of the universe are such that anything that is not in harmony with that purity and light simply disintegrates. Evil is not allowed to exist in these sublime regions; it is driven out. It can exist only in the lower regions where it is free to roam, creating havoc and making people miserable, because it is only in the lower regions of matter that it finds the conditions it needs. So, depending on the region in which you dwell, evil may or may not be able to reach you. This is what Initiatic Science teaches.

---

* Related reading: *Angels and other Mysteries of the Tree of Life,* Izvor No. 236.

** See plate and note on pp. 398 to 401.

9 October

Every human being is accompanied by invisible entities.* If these entities are benevolent, they clear difficulties from our path; but if they are malevolent, they try to foil every attempt to do something useful or constructive and do their best to steer us into a blind alley. When a king goes somewhere, he is preceded by servants who prepare the way; when he arrives, everything is ready, simply because he is the king. Whereas who thinks about preparing the way for a beggar?

The same rules apply in our inner life: the path of those who are kings or queens is smooth and free of obstacles, and lined with crowds of people ready to welcome them. Whereas, those who are beggars – who are inwardly poor in virtues – will not be welcomed anywhere. The secret of true life lies in achieving only one thing: dominion over oneself, seeking to be a monarch in perfect control of their thoughts, feelings and actions. Those who are truly masters of their own kingdom are always preceded by invisible entities who prepare the best conditions for them.

* Related reading: *Toward a Solar Civilization,* Izvor No. 201, Chaps. 2, 6, 8 and 9.

10 October

Light* cannot enter the mind of someone whose curtains are drawn. If you keep your curtains closed, light will be shut out. Light has the power to set worlds in motion, that is true, but it still cannot open your curtains for you; you must do that yourself.

As soon as they are open, light will suddenly come pouring into your room – that is, into your head and into your mind. Then, when your inner being is flooded with light and you understand just how a luminous thought can sanctify objects and creatures, you must undertake to work in this way so that, from morning to night, you may live in the extraordinary joy of sanctifying everything you touch or lay eyes on.

* Related reading: *Light is a Living Spirit,* Izvor No. 212.

11 October

When you leave this world, each one of you will go to live in whichever region you have aspired to during your life on earth. If your aspirations were very elevated, you will go to a region of light;* but if they were vile and base, you will go to a region of darkness. Your destiny depends on your proper understanding of this law. If your heart yearns only for intelligence, love or beauty, you can be absolutely sure that nothing will have the power to prevent you from reaching the region of your aspirations.

When human beings believe that they have only this one earthly life to live, they are ready to use all kinds of dishonest and criminal means to satisfy their desires – and they think that they are doing very well for themselves with their crooked ways. In fact, they are sadly mistaken: through ignorance, they are preparing terrible suffering for themselves in the next world.

* Related reading: *'Walk While You Have the Light'*, Izvor No. 244, Chaps. 7, 14 and 15.

12 October

Jesus said, *'The kingdom of God is at hand.'** Many people will point out that two thousand years have gone by since he said this, and the kingdom of God still seems to be a long way off. There are so many wars, so much famine, poverty and misery in the world!

We must interpret Jesus' words and understand what he meant when he said that the kingdom of God was near. For some, it has already come; yes, it is already within the hearts and souls of those who were ready to receive it, who were able to accept and apply his teaching of love. For others, it is close, it is coming. And for a third category, it will come, but we cannot tell when. So the kingdom of God has come, is coming and will come – all three statements are true.

* Related reading: *The True Meaning of Christ's Teaching,* Izvor No. 215 and *Looking into the Invisible,* Izvor No. 228.

13 October

Many Christians believe that their faith* will save them. No, that would be too easy; anybody can believe and yet continue to behave like a criminal. Many criminals say they believe in God, but that will not save them. Faith that is not accompanied by the corresponding attitudes and actions – or, at least, by an effort in that direction – is almost worthless. Faith is truly powerful only when it is followed by actions that conform to one's beliefs.

Take a very simple example: you believe in the effectiveness of a medicine, but if you do not take it, it will not do you any good. On the other hand, if you do take it, your faith will make it twice, three times, ten times as potent as it would be if you had no faith in it. Faith is not everything; it simply opens doors and windows and clears the path ahead for you. But if you make no effort to walk that path, you will remain stuck in front of the open door.

* Related reading: *The Faith that Moves Mountains,* Izvor No. 238 and *Love Greater than Faith,* Izvor No. 239.

14 October

We all have a goal in life, and the goal of a spiritual Master is not to attract everybody to himself, but to train workers to work for the coming of the kingdom of God. So, if he senses that by his teaching he is not training genuine workers, true servants of God, he will have the impression that he has been wasting his time, that his work has been for nothing.

His disciples would do well to think, 'Our Master* is there to help, enlighten and instruct us, to link us with heaven, but isn't there something we should be doing for him? Doesn't he, too, have certain wishes and aspirations?' And they will find that he does indeed want something. But the difference is that he does not want anything for himself. He wants workers who will spread light, servants of God who will work for the good of the whole world.

* Related reading: *What is a Spiritual Master?*, Izvor No. 207 and *Life with the Master Peter Deunov,* Autobiographical Reflections 2.

15 October

'*When God drew a circle on the face of the deep, I was there,*' says Wisdom, in the *Book of Proverbs*. What is this circle?* It is the boundary drawn by God himself in order to create the world. So in this sense we can say that to create, God limited himself. To limit oneself means to enclose oneself in a universe that functions and evolves according to its own laws, to have no knowledge of what exists outside or beyond that universe. The laws of life that are the object of scientific study are simply the limits that God imposed upon himself in his creation. These limits are what give matter its structure, form, shape and cohesion. A world that was not circumscribed by limits would be unstable. It could not endure, because all the matter within those limits is in motion, perpetually seeking to burst its bonds.

God drew a circle in order to restrain his own substance. The circle is a magical outline. God placed the seed of creation in the centre of this circle, and his work began.

* Related reading: *The Zodiac, Key to Man and to the Universe,* Izvor No. 220.

16 October

*F*orms always have a tendency to become rigid,* and when human beings do not guard against this, the spirit that animates these forms is no longer able to manifest its presence. It has to go and look for new forms, more suited to what it wants to express.

This law is valid in every area, even in religion. The Christian Church, for example, is wrong to have insisted on clinging to the same forms for centuries. It has not understood that forms have to be continually refined and diversified, so that they can express the ever-new currents of the spirit more and more perfectly. It is human beings who are attached to forms; Cosmic Intelligence has not designed them to be immutable. Human beings may well refuse to allow forms to evolve, but events will always occur to upend and shatter rites and doctrines that were thought to be eternal. What human beings think is not what Cosmic Intelligence thinks – Cosmic Intelligence has other plans. This is why there will now be upheavals in the world, which the spirit will use to show human beings that they must not try to confine it.

---

* Related reading: *'In Spirit and in Truth'*, Izvor No. 235, Chaps. 11 and 12, and *'Walk While You Have the Light'*, Izvor No. 244, Chap. 8.

17 October

For thousands of years, Initiates have studied the breathing process* and have come to understand its importance, not only for our physical vitality, but also for the function of our thought. They went so far with their studies that they came to see that all the rhythms of the human organism are related to cosmic rhythms. They discovered that in order to communicate with a particular entity or region of the spiritual world, human beings must find the appropriate rhythm, make it their own, and use it as a key, exactly as one does to tune into a radio station by finding the right wavelength.

The wavelength is an essential factor in making contact with a broadcasting station, and the same is true of breathing: you have to know with what rhythm to breathe in order to make contact with a particular region of the universe.

* Related reading: *Harmony and Health,* Izvor No. 225, Chaps. 4 to 7 (particularly Chaps. 5 and 6).

18 October

When you love somebody, do not be in too much of a hurry to tell them. It is better that they should not know. It is your love that makes you happy, that stimulates you and gives meaning to your life,* and as the one you love is not perfect, if they know how you feel, there is a danger that without meaning to, they may ruin everything. They will think to themselves, 'Ah, the door is open – let's make the most of it!' Yes, it is only natural. But later, when you feel that they do not understand you, you will suffer, you will be disappointed and your love will die. And that is a pity, for it is love that gives you wings. You must not sacrifice it for someone who may well destroy it.

So love, but keep your love well hidden. There will be time enough to talk about it when you are both strong and fully prepared. In the meantime, say nothing. What matters is to go on loving. Never forget that it is your love that is important, more important than whom you love. You must never lose that love, for it is this that nourishes you and gives you your ardour, your zest for life, the will to overcome all obstacles.

* Related reading: *Sexual Force or the Winged Dragon*, Izvor No. 205, Chaps. 2, 4 and 6.

19 October

The things you achieve on the physical plane are there for all to see and touch, whereas nobody can see your spiritual achievements – not even you. The lack of tangible proof of your work may lead you to doubt and make you want to abandon your spiritual practices and devote yourself solely to activities that can offer you some visible results. Do as you wish but, one day, even in the midst of great success, you will sense that something vital is missing inside. This is only to be expected, for you have still not touched on what is essential, you have not yet sown anything in the realm of light, wisdom, love or eternity.

Only your inner, spiritual achievements can give you a sense of fulfilment, for only they put down roots within you. And when you leave this earth, you will take with you, in your heart and soul and spirit, the precious stones – that is, the qualities and virtues – that you have worked to develop, and your name will be inscribed in the book of eternal life.*

* Related reading: *The Powers of Thought,* Izvor No. 224, Chap. 1.

20 October

It is easy to explain why human beings hold certain opinions or behave in certain ways. It is even easy to understand that they make mistakes and do all kinds of stupid things. But to claim that their opinions and actions correspond to the truth is another matter. Individuals form their opinions depending on their faculties, capacities, temperament and needs, that is all. How presumptuous they are when they say, 'I believe this… I don't believe that', as though they were proclaiming an eternal truth! As though their belief or unbelief were enough to make it true or untrue!

The important thing is not to believe or disbelieve, but to study, to verify, for this is how we get closer to the truth. Do those who say, 'I believe,' know why they believe? What has inspired their belief? Human beings believe a great many things because it suits them, because it is to their advantage – it corresponds to their needs, their sensibilities or their interests. Well, they can believe whatever they like, they have the right to do so, but they must not imagine that what they believe is the truth. Above all, they should stop trying to impose their beliefs on others!

21 October

Nothing can match the speed of light, which shows that it is the most perfect of all God's creatures. Yes, speed is a measure of perfection. When your thoughts become sluggish, you cannot count on them to give you a quick and accurate view of the situation or the way to deal with it, and you may have an accident or fall into a trap. Similarly, when your inner, psychic life slows down, everything becomes more difficult: you feel ill at ease and lose your zest for life.

Light is a yardstick, a criterion.* As it is pure, disinterested and free of all burdens, light wins every race and slips in everywhere. If you wish to explore the human heart, the universe and all the treasures of the universal Soul, try inwardly to achieve the speed and intensity of light.

* Related reading: *Light is a Living Spirit,* Izvor No. 212, Chap. 8.

22 October

Whenever some new event or situation crops up, take the time to consider both sides of the matter. Do not focus exclusively on the negative aspects.* Of course, I am not saying that we should delude ourselves by always saying that everything that happens is good, but we must refuse to dwell only on the bad aspects. You probably think that this advice is not exactly new, that you know all that already... Well, if you know it, put it into practice!

Observe yourselves and you will see that you often forget this rule and give in to unhappiness and pessimism. In doing so, not only do you fail to reason correctly, but you also prevent your soul from blossoming and taking flight. This is how you destroy yourselves spiritually and even physically. Yes, why do we colloquially say that worry 'is eating away' or 'gnawing' at someone who is constantly anxious and dissatisfied?

* Related reading: *The Wellsprings of Eternal Joy,* Izvor No. 242, Chap. 5.

23 October

Christians recite, *'In the name of the Father, the Son, and the Holy Ghost'** and they never seem surprised that there is no mention of a feminine principle in this trinity. Yet we cannot help but wonder. When you hear, 'father and on' – words that evoke the notion of a family – is it not strange that the third member of this family should be the Holy Ghost? What kind of family has no mother? The Kabbalists are right when they teach that God has a wife, whom they call Shekhinah.

Christians must accept the existence of this cosmic principle, the feminine dimension of the creative principle. The being that we call God – and that Christianity sees as a masculine force – is, in reality, both masculine and feminine. Before there can be creation or manifestation, there must be polarization, that is, the presence of a masculine principle and a feminine principle. In order to manifest, God has to be both masculine and feminine. This is what was also taught in the Orphic initiations: God is male and female.

* Related reading: *Toward a Solar Civilization,* Izvor No. 201, Chap. 9.

24 October

When you leave your home in the morning, remember to greet all the creatures of the visible and invisible worlds. By this simple gesture* you will create a link with them, and for the rest of the day you will live in an atmosphere of poetry and light. You send out your love and then love comes back to you from every corner of the universe.

There are so many ways of making life beautiful and poetic! But you must take care not to let yourself be overwhelmed by worries and material matters, so that you have time and energy for the activities that can give more meaning to your life. Human beings still do not understand this: they talk about love and long to be loved, but they remain closed off, drab and prosaic. If they would only learn to live poetically, they would be loved.

* Related reading: *The Book of Divine Magic,* Izvor No. 226, Chap. 12.

25 October

*M*atter is inert and formless until the spirit descends into it to bring it to life. The vivifying spirit is symbolized by a point, and matter by the circle that surrounds it. Cosmic Intelligence has placed this figure of a point surrounded by a circle* throughout the universe. We see it in fruit (the flesh that surrounds a core or seed), in our eyes, in certain parts of men's and women's anatomy. It even corresponds to the structure of a cell, of an atom and of the solar system... We see this symbol everywhere we look, for it represents the whole of life, the whole of creation: in the centre of the circle is the point, the Cosmic Spirit that vivifies the universe.

Initiates, who understand the potency of this symbol, ask only to possess this point – the spirit – within themselves. And we too are circles; each one of us must ask to receive the central point, the Holy Spirit. As long as we remain a circle without a point, we will be empty and unfulfilled. But the day the central point, the Spirit, comes to dwell within us to animate and illuminate us, we shall be fulfilled.

* Related reading: *The Symbolic Language of Geometrical Figures,* Izvor No. 218, Chap. 2.

26 October

*T*rue sensitivity is complete openness to the divine world, that is, to beauty, love and truth, and a closed door to what is negative and obscure. The thin-skinned touchiness that makes people acutely aware of insults and offences is not true sensitivity. What is left for all the poor wretches for whom heaven, the angels, friends and beauty simply do not exist, except for the wicked and unjust people about whom they spend their time complaining?

You must not confuse sensitivity and touchiness;* touchiness is an unhealthy manifestation of sensitivity. True sensitivity, on the other hand, is a high degree of evolution that opens us to the heavenly realms and enables us to attune ourselves to their vibrations.

* Related reading: *The Seeds of Happiness,* Izvor No. 231, Chap. 10.

27 October

*T*ruth is always very simple. For the Initiates, everything is simple, because they have learned to reduce the infinite multiplicity of facts and situations on the physical and psychic planes to a few basic principles.

What are these principles? Geometrical figures. Yes, does that surprise you? Why do you suppose some of the ancient philosophical traditions spoke of God as the great geometer? Plato himself says that God works with geometry. At the origin of these traditions are the great minds who understood that the multiplicity of beings and objects and their mutual relationships could be reduced to the very simple principles expressed by geometrical figures* such as a circle, triangle, square, pyramid, cross and so on.

* Related reading: *The Symbolic Language of Geometrical Figures,* Izvor No. 218.

28 October

A mere breath can blow out the flame of a candle, but if you feed that flame, the breath that once threatened to extinguish it will make it so powerful that nothing can put it out. A flame is a symbol of the spirit.* If you do not nourish your spirit, if you neglect it because you supposedly have better things to do, the flame of your spirit will become so weak that the slightest little difficulty can snuff it out.

There are many people whose spirit has been snuffed out: they drag themselves through life, they eat and drink and potter about, but their spirit is no longer alight. Others, on the contrary, continue to nourish their spirit by means of prayer, meditation and contemplation, and it becomes so strong that the storms of life only make it burn more brightly. Yes, the difficulties and obstacles that strike down the weak serve to strengthen the children of the spirit. But you must not rely on the spirit, thinking, 'Oh, the spirit is so strong and powerful that it will come to help me when I'm in trouble'. No, the spirit is not yet strong and powerful, but it will be extremely powerful provided you nourish it.

* Related reading: *The Mysteries of Fire and Water,* Izvor No. 232, Chaps. 9, 13, 14 and 17.

29 October

What do you do when it rains or hails, when a storm and high winds are raging? Do you go out and fight the elements? No, you look after your house: you fill in the cracks, replace broken tiles, make sure that it is well insulated, and so on. Once your house is shored up and secure you can rest easy. You know very well what to do when it comes to the forces of nature, so how is it that where evil is concerned, you no longer know what to do? You believe that you can vanquish evil by attacking it head-on, but you are the one who will be vanquished. Instead of battling evil, you must make yourself stronger so as to be able to resist better, understand better and take better action.

Even Archangel Michael did not destroy evil,* for it is written in *Revelation* that he did not slay the dragon, he merely put it in chains and subdued it. So how can we, who are so much less powerful than Archangel Michael, believe that if we fight against evil we will succeed in destroying it?

* Related reading: *The Tree of the Knowledge of Good and Evil,* Izvor No. 210, Chap. 3 and *Truth, Fruit of Wisdom and Love,* Izvor No. 234, Chap. 17.

30 October

It is said that before creating the world, God first drew its boundaries. Everything in nature confirms this, starting with a cell and its membrane. And if the skull did not exist, where would our brain be? This is exactly the function of our skin too – it serves as a boundary.

Observe the things around you: wherever you look, you will see a reflection of the circle that God drew in order to circumscribe his creation. If perfume is not sealed in a bottle, it evaporates. Even when you build a house, you have to begin with the frame, for if there were no walls, where would your house be? We have to understand how boundaries apply in the spiritual realm too. Before summoning spirits of light to help him in his work, a magus surrounds himself with a circle; and disciples also know that, if only through thought, they must draw a circle of light* around themselves so as to preserve their spiritual energies.

* Related reading: *The Book of Divine Magic,* Izvor No. 226, Chap. 2.

31 October

Look at people coming and going in the streets of a city: they mingle, their paths cross, and yet each one goes their separate way, bent exclusively on their own business. There is no cohesion and, consequently, no power in a crowd such as this. But then, from the milling crowd, emerges a man who begins to speak with such determination and assurance that the passers-by gather round and listen. In some cases, drawn by the strength of his convictions, they follow him and espouse his cause. As soon as a head, a leader appears, everyone immediately rallies around him – then what strength, what power the crowd takes on.

Well, this is an image of what can happen within you. Your life seems to have no meaning, because all your organs, all the cells of your body, are in disarray and without cohesion, everything is too scattered and displaced. Make up your minds to stand up and talk to the population that inhabits you, and persuade them to follow you on a divine path. The motto 'Strength in unity' should not apply only to a country or a society, but to every human being. Human beings must awaken the forces present in their consciousness, their subconsciousness and the cells of their body, and marshal them in the service of one central idea, so that the image of God lying deep within them may shine forth.

1 November

It is good to get into the habit of periodically taking stock of our lives. Why? Because, all too often the lives we lead, day in, day out become weighed down and clouded by all kinds of concerns and activities that contribute nothing spiritual to our lives.

Subjected to the influences that surround us, we forget that our time on earth is very short, and that all our material possessions, titles and social rank must be left behind. You will say that we all know this. Yes, everybody knows, but everybody forgets; even disciples of an initiatic school are swayed by the influences around them. That is why it is vital that we take the time every now and again to look back over our lives, analyze the direction we are taking and the activities in which we are engaged, so that we can sort through them and keep only what is essential.*

* Related reading: *Harmony and Health,* Izvor No. 225, Chap. 1.

2 November

It is normal to feel antipathy towards certain people, because human beings cannot possess that universal consciousness which would allow them to attune themselves with everything and everyone. We shall always experience some aversions, be it to certain foods, objects, faces or behaviour. When we come to earth, we take on a body in some family or other and this body does not vibrate in perfect harmony with the whole universe and all living creatures.

But should we allow this state of affairs to be our guiding principle? No. Obviously, it is easier to seek out only what is pleasant. But if we listen to the voice of wisdom that sees things differently, it will advise against acting only according to our likes and dislikes. Why not widen our horizons, seeking what is good not only for ourselves, but for others too? We must finally get a grip on this capricious nature of ours, which loves this and detests that, instead of being forever at its beck and call. Many people have taken a fall through living only according to personal tastes and tendencies!

3 November

*T*he foremost task of an educator is to awaken in children a sense of the divine world and of the hierarchy of celestial creatures ascending all the way to the throne of God. Yes, it is essential to instil in the souls and spirits of the younger generation the idea that a sublime world exists, to which they can turn for strength, courage and inspiration, not only in difficulties and trials, but in all circumstances of daily life as well.

Of course, you should not expect young people to know and relate to the divine world immediately, even if they have been instructed in the truths of Initiatic Science. No, but they will always be able to draw on spiritual resources through this connection they will have learned to establish with heaven, and an inner world of great riches and power will always be at their disposal. And at times when other young people may despair, break down, or succumb to criminal ways, they will advance, improve and become wonderful examples.*

* Related reading: *Education Begins Before Birth,* Izvor No. 203, Chap. 11.

4 November

*E*very activity produces combustion. Whether that activity be physical, emotional or intellectual, it results in the formation of waste matter that must be rejected, for the build-up creates congestion that is detrimental to the proper functioning of the organism. For example, when we want to light a fire in a stove, if we do not first remove the old cinders, the flames will not catch, and the stove will not work. The same is true for our physical body and also our psychic body – the realm of thoughts and feelings.

So that is why we must improve our whole way of life, that is, the way we eat, think, feel and love, because in this way we replace the waste matter with other substances that are far more subtle, light and etheric. This is how we feed our inner fire in order to continue our work.*

* Related reading: *The Second Birth,* Complete Works Vol. 1, Chap. I.

5 November

Instead of providing humanity with comfort and weapons, pandering to human instincts of laziness and aggression, science should orient its research in another direction. Can scientists be happy or proud to have given us so many increasingly efficient ways to destroy ourselves? As human beings move towards total self-destruction, they are also gradually losing their physical stamina and mental faculties, because of all the devices that relieve them of any effort.

It seems as though progress is being made, but in reality our willpower and our spiritual faculties are diminishing. This is why more and more thinkers and even scientists have begun to question whether all this technical progress is really helping humanity. This does not mean that progress should be halted. No, it is nature itself that drives human beings to do research, but this research must be given a different direction. We must never stop searching, never cease delving into the mysteries of nature, but simply take a different direction, toward the heights, toward the spirit.*

* Related reading: *The Yoga of Nutrition,* Izvor No. 204, Chap. 4.

6 November

*A*llow only one anarchic idea to enter your mind and little by little this idea will spread disorder through your entire being, right down to the soles of your feet. This is how we end up becoming veritable battlefields. Initiates fear, above all else, to disturb the cosmic order established by the Creator, because they know that one day they would themselves be a victim of the resulting disorder. It is extraordinary that, although this makes Initiates tremble, ordinary people remain calm, confident, even daring. Of course they can be audacious because they are so ignorant of the dangers. Many people, attempting to prove their independence, behave like anarchists! They do not know that real strength is compliance with divine laws.

All our happiness, all our future success is based on the respect of the sublime order established by God, and submitted to by angels, archangels and all heavenly entities – but not by human beings! This respect for the divine hierarchy is the fundamental principle of an initiatic teaching.

7 November

Initiates need to nourish themselves just like everybody else, but what they seek is the divine life. When they find fruits and flowers – that is, human beings who carry this divine life within them – they pause by them and say to themselves, 'Thank you heavenly Father, thank you divine Mother, I can see aspects of you within these people. By means of these fruits and flowers, I can now draw closer to you and contemplate you. Through this splendour I can breathe in your fragrance and savour your delights.' And they go away happy, because these fruits and flowers have brought them closer to heaven.*

* Related reading: *The Yoga of Nutrition,* Izvor No. 204, Chap. 11.

8 November

Human beings are absorbed with all sorts of projects, but to what end? It is very, very rare that their efforts are directed toward becoming a servant of God, a conductor of light. It would be easy to provide them with the means to do so, but it is far more difficult to make them aspire to such an ideal. Even the Lord cannot give them this desire. This deep longing has to come from people themselves – nobody else can desire in your stead, just as nobody else can feel hungry and eat on your behalf.

A Master can give you all the necessary food, metaphorically speaking, but you are the ones who must eat it; the Master cannot eat it for you. If a Master eats on your behalf, he will get 'fatter', and you will get 'thinner'! A Master gives you knowledge, but the willingness to accept and apply it must come from you. Your Master's knowledge, together with your own good will, will produce astonishing results.*

* Related reading: *What is a Spiritual Master?*, Izvor No. 207, Chap. 2.

9 November

Human beings always manage things in such a way that what could be used for their salvation or the salvation of others ultimately serves only to ruin them. Why is this? A lack of enlightenment, greed and the need to control. Look at how many researchers regret revealing the results of their work, because their discoveries immediately fell into the hands of people who misused them to harm their fellow human beings, to dominate, destroy or exploit them.

Even Initiates and spiritual Masters have always been very careful about this, because they realized that the great truths they revealed to help humans could be turned around and used to lead people to their downfall. This is why they gave the precept: 'Know, will, dare and keep silent.'* When human beings are more evolved, more revelations will be possible. Meanwhile, it is often better to keep quiet and accept the advice of Jesus not to *'throw pearls before swine'*.

* Related reading: *What is a Spiritual Master?*, Izvor No. 207, Chap. 3.

10 November

In the Scriptures, God is called the Most High, because power is inseparable from the idea of height, of the summit. Even in battle, it is easier to conquer an enemy if we occupy a higher position. In a lower position, we are always more vulnerable and certainly weaker. This law is also important to know for our spiritual life; otherwise, we could work for years with no results.

When you want to meditate, the first step is to calm your astral and mental bodies.* As you gradually extricate yourself from fog, noise and dust – that is, as you move out of the lower astral and mental planes – your thought gains strength. When you sense that your mind soars high in etheric regions, know that this is where the real work begins, work that will produce results.**

* See note and diagram on pp. 396 and 397.

** Related reading: *Man's Psychic Life: Elements and Structures,* Izvor No. 222, Chap. 10.

11 November

Every form, every physical manifestation has its origin in the invisible world.* Every thought, feeling and emotion that arises in us gradually assumes the specific shape corresponding to its nature, leaving visible marks upon our faces and bodies. Our thoughts and feelings act first upon the most secret vibrations of our being, then on our emanations, then on our skin, then on our fragrance, and finally upon the shape of our bodies. That is how our current faces and bodies were formed and determined: by all the inner states through which we have lived in previous existences.

Disciples, who know that they are the sculptors of their own body, work upon it through thoughts and feelings to make of it a temple, harmonious in form and proportion.

* Related reading: *Know Thyself' – Jnana Yoga (Part I),* Complete Works Vol. 17, Chap. IX.

12 November

Someone comes and complains that he is very unhappy. I ask him, 'Have you given thanks today?'

'Given thanks! To whom? What for?'

'Can you walk and breathe?'

'Yes...'

'Have you had something to eat?'

'Yes...'

'And can you open your mouth to speak?'

'Yes...'

'Very well then, thank the Lord. There are people who can neither walk, nor eat, nor even open their mouths. You are miserable because it has never occurred to you to give thanks. In order to change your frame of mind, you would first have to realize that nothing is more wonderful than to be alive, able to walk, look and speak.' But human beings forget all this, which is why heaven puts them through great hardships – to teach them finally to be grateful.*

* Related reading: *The Laughter of a Sage,* Izvor No. 243, Chap. 12.

13 November

*A*t its origin, at the beginning of all things, there is light. And this light is the Christ, the solar Spirit. The spirit of the Christ first manifests in the sephirah *Chokmah,* the highest glory, the Word, without which, as Saint John says in his Gospel, 'nothing was made'. It then manifests under another aspect in the sephirah *Tiphareth,* the sun.*

That is why when you go to watch the sun rising each morning, consider that as you link yourself with it, you are uniting with its spirit; yes, with the spirit of the sun, which is none other than the spirit of Christ, an emanation of God Himself. It is not enough just to be there and gaze at it: to have true contact with the quintessence of its light, your spirit must link with it and enter into it. As soon as you plunge into that world of light, a few particles of light penetrate within you and you receive revelations of divine splendour.**

* See plate and note on pp. 398 to 401.

** Related reading: *The Splendour of Tiphareth – The Yoga of the Sun,* Complete Works Vol. 10, Chap. X.

14 November

We need a method to guide us in our spiritual work and point out the best path to follow. For me, the best method of all is the study of the Sephirotic Tree, the Tree of Life,* and that is why I insist that you learn to deepen your knowledge of all its aspects.

With *Malkuth* you give things material form. With *Yesod* you purify them. With *Hod* you understand and express them. With *Netzach* you give them grace. With *Tiphareth* you bring light to them. With *Geburah* you fight to defend them. With *Chesed* you submit them to divine order. With *Binah* you give them stability. With *Chokmah* you bring them into universal harmony. Finally, with *Kether* you place the seal of eternity upon them.**

* See plate and note on pp. 398 to 401.

** Related reading: *Angels and other Mysteries of the Tree of Life,* Izvor No. 236, Chap. 2.

15 November

Difficulties and trials are necessary in order for us to advance, grow and become stronger. People who choose an easy existence for fear of suffering are wasting their life force, and they will be obliged to pass through other ordeals.

The grain of wheat that hides away in the granary, believing itself to be safe, will be eaten by mice or will grow mouldy. But the grain of wheat that reasons, 'I do not want to stay here doing nothing, I want to become a fine ear of corn, so please sow me in the ground', will be put into the earth. Of course, when it finds itself in the cold and dark it will cry, 'I did not ask for this treatment!' But it will sprout. Later, at harvest time, it will be cut down and will again complain loudly. And when it is threshed and separated from the straw, it will bitterly bewail the cruelty of its fate. And that is not the end of it: one day it will be carted off to the mill to be ground, then kneaded with water, and after that put into the oven. What a life! But when it is placed on the table, well baked and golden brown, to be feasted upon by beautiful, good people, this grain of wheat will finally understand why it had to go through all these trials, and it will be happy.

So, stay quietly in your granary if you so wish, but your life will be a useless one.

16 November

Human beings can become messengers of the invisible world if they adopt a receptive attitude. However, great vigilance is needed, because if they become too receptive they will be like sponges, absorbing everything, both good and bad. People tend to think that the invisible world is inhabited solely by luminous and beneficent beings, but this is not so. Just as people on earth vary between good and bad, so malicious entities also inhabit the invisible world, and as they are often very hostile to us, they love to lead us astray, or torment us.

So be prudent, and do not lay yourselves totally open to the invisible world. If you have not already worked to obtain the purity and higher level of awareness needed to repulse the attacks of dark forces, you must be active and vigilant.*

* Related reading: *Looking into the Invisible,* Izvor No. 228, Chap. 1.

17 November

It is true that you will meet with difficulties, and that people are often mean and ungrateful, but is that a reason to be always outraged, indignant and bitter? In the end, you are the one to suffer from this attitude. People may say, 'But I am free to do as I like, as long as I am hurting only myself and nobody else.' Well, this proves how little they understand.

We are all linked to each other, and our moods of sadness, depression and darkness are reflected on those around us. You do not wish to hurt anyone? On the face of it, this is true but, in fact, your behaviour spreads negative emanations and particles that are harmful to other people. You are mistaken if you believe that you are separate from other people, for your thoughts and feelings act on your parents and friends, and even on the animals, plants and objects around you. By hurting yourself, you are hurting the whole world.*

* Related reading: *A Philosophy of Universality,* Izvor No. 206, Chap. 6.

18 November

When you feel weighed down by worries and sorrow, look up at the starry night sky and reflect on how tiny this earth is within the infinity of space. Consider how the One who created so many worlds must surely have peopled them with beings far more intelligent, beautiful and powerful than us. For when we see how these puny humans argue, bicker and slaughter each other, how can we believe that the earth – a mere speck of dust in the immensity of space – is where the Creator has placed the most perfect beings in existence?

Beneath the stars, all the problems that take on such gigantic proportions in your minds come to seem infinitesimal. Remembering that these stars have been in existence for billions of years, that the Intelligence that created this world is eternal, and that you are created in the same image, you feel your spirit to be eternal, too, and understand that nothing can really trouble you.*

* Related reading: *Know Thyself' – Jnana Yoga (Part I)*, Complete Works Vol. 17, Chap. VI.

19 November

When we speak about 'attention', we must know that this word can be interpreted in several ways. Usually, of course, it means that sustained focus we all need in order to do our work properly, to understand what has been said to us, or to read a book, and so on. However, there is another form of attention known as self-awareness or introspection. This entails a constant awareness of all our inner goings-on, of all passing currents, desires and thoughts, of all the influences and conflicts we experience. It is this attention that is not sufficiently developed.

The Scriptures say, *'Be vigilant, because the devil, like a roaring lion, is ready to devour you.'* Rest assured that you will not see a lion or the devil on the physical plane; the threat lies in the inner realm. It is there that desires, plans, passions and cravings seek to swallow you up, and you must be very attentive or you will be devoured.*

* Related reading: *Golden Rules for Everyday Life,* Izvor No. 227, Chap. 18.

20 November

In order to gain access to some places you need a pass, and as soon as you have it, the doors open to let you in. It is exactly the same in the invisible world: we need a pass to enter each region, and these passes are the different colours in our aura. So, to gain entrance into a specific region, our aura must have the colour that will open the door to that region. If, for example, you have yellow in your aura, you will gain entry to the libraries of nature where all its secrets will be revealed to you. Blue will take you into the realm of music, and red will give access to the region in which you can draw upon the very essence of vitality.

The deciding factor for permission to enter the invisible world is, therefore, the aura, and the colours it contains are passes to the corresponding regions.*

* Related reading: *Man's Subtle Bodies and Centres,* Izvor No. 219, Chap. 2.

21 November

One day, a young man went to visit a Master, hoping to be accepted as his disciple. So the lesson began, and this was the Master's first instruction: 'Take a walk around the cemetery, hurl insults at the dead, listen carefully to what they reply, and then report back to me.' The young man went to the cemetery and wandered round among the graves, giving voice to dreadful insults – corpses in a cemetery had never heard the like before! He soon ran dry of insults, so he stopped and listened: no reply. Returning to the Master, he had to admit that the dead had failed to react. 'Ah,' said the Master, 'perhaps they were offended. Go back again, but this time try praising them, and perhaps they will decide to respond to that.' So the young man went back to the cemetery, and – change of tune – began singing their praises. Nothing. Silence. Utterly dejected, the young man returned to the Master and confessed, 'They still haven't answered me.' 'Well,' replied the Master, 'now you must learn to be like them: whether you are insulted or praised, you must remain unmoved; you must not reply.'*

* Related reading: *The Second Birth,* Complete Works Vol. 1, Chap. VI.

22 November

An angel is an immortal creature made of matter so pure and subtle that nothing can harm it. Angels dwell in light and perfect joy and have knowledge of everything except suffering. For suffering can affect only matter that is not absolutely pure – angels cannot suffer because they are absolutely pure.

Angels do not exist on the physical plane, they are to be found only in the higher regions of the astral plane and above.* At the boundary between the lower and the higher astral plane there is an intermediary zone inhabited by beings who are in the process of severing their bonds with the regions of darkness. They can still be tormented by the negative influences of the lower astral and physical planes, but once they have worked their way through this zone, they will become like angels.**

* See note and diagram on pp. 396 and 397.

** Related reading: *The Mysteries of Yesod,* Complete Works Vol. 7, Chap. I.

23 November

*M*any artists, whether painters, musicians, poets, novelists or playwrights, have destroyed some of their works in fits of discouragement, even though these may have been of great merit! That is a pity, because in doing so they harmed themselves and deprived the whole world of their masterpieces as well. The reason for their action is that they remained too focused on themselves, on their own difficulties and problems. Not knowing how to extricate themselves from the limits of their ego, they failed to connect with all that is good and beautiful in people and in nature. Only this attitude could have protected them and prevented them from turning against their works in a fit of dissatisfaction.

Truly spiritual people are not satisfied with themselves, but they find happiness in the works of God and marvel at those who serve Him and in this way, they remedy the sorrow caused by their own imperfections.*

* Related reading: *Harmony and Health,* Izvor No. 225, Chap. 9.

24 November

No phenomenon, thought, feeling or action can exist in isolation, without being linked to another phenomenon, thought, feeling or action. Each has a cause, and each, sooner or later, produces consequences. Every day of your life provides examples of this.

Suppose you have had a good day; then, just as you are going to bed, something happens that saddens or disheartens you. As you awaken the following morning, it is obvious that all the happiness of the previous day has been erased, replaced by these few disagreeable moments just as you fell asleep, and this unpleasant impression remains. This means that the last moment was more important and more significant than all the rest of the day.*

* Related reading: *Looking into the Invisible,* Izvor No. 228, Chap. 14.

25 November

Human beings are inhabited by 'workers', and as we cross from wakefulness into sleep, these workers use everything within us as materials, as constructive or destructive forces. This is why you must be vigilant as you go to bed, avoiding all states of irritation and discouragement, because these states of mind set to work, they are entities that not only destroy all the good you have acquired during the day, but that also prepare poor conditions for the next day.

So, take care to conjure up at least one light-filled thought, one feeling of love, one inspiring image before you go to sleep, and you will wake up the following morning feeling purified and restored.*

* Related reading: *Looking into the Invisible,* Izvor No. 228, Chap. 14.

26 November

*T*eaching is the highest and most noble of all professions. Of course, not everyone shares this opinion: becoming a lawyer, engineer or doctor is considered to be very worthwhile indeed, whereas caring for children is of no significance. Yet this is the most important, meaningful occupation of all, with enormous consequences for the future. Bringing up children is such a responsibility – for teachers and parents alike. It is divine work. This is why there will come a day when psychology and child education will be held in the highest regard despite the fact that now they are still looked down upon. And that day is fast approaching. Attention is increasingly turning to these subjects: the human being, psychological life, upbringing and education.

The history of humankind shows clearly that problems can be truly resolved only when psychology and pedagogy are given first place.

27 November

In initiatic science, a horse represents our lower nature – our personality – which expresses itself through the physical, astral and mental bodies.* So for disciples, the first task is to learn to control their horse or, more precisely, their team of horses. They must know how to handle the reins. What are these reins? They are the fluidic links the rider establishes between himself and his three horses, enabling him to guide them in the right direction.

But for the horses to obey and pull together harmoniously, they must be well nourished with the appropriate food. If you wish to train your physical horse – your body – you must provide healthy, fresh food and exercise to make it strong. The astral horse can be tamed only by means of purity, love and gentleness. Finally, the mental horse must be nourished only with intelligence and light.**

* See note and diagram on pp. 396 and 397.

** Related reading: *The Zodiac, Key to Man and to the Universe,* Izvor No. 220, Chap. 10.

*H*onesty, kindness, generosity, patience, peace, harmony and brotherhood will be the most highly esteemed values of the new life. Those who do not know how to manifest these virtues will be considered useless, even harmful. Diplomas will be awarded to those whose behaviour serves to bring peace and harmony, and not to those who are simply like a walking encyclopaedia.

Strong characters are needed to bring the kingdom of God to earth, not information services. In fact, real diplomas are awarded by nature, and nature alone. If the mere touch of your hand can bring relief to someone who is troubled and distressed, that is proof that heaven has awarded you a diploma. Do you possess a gift, a talent or a virtue? It is a diploma granted by the Lord. True diplomas are not pieces of paper; they are imprinted on your face and body – in the fibre of your whole being. You may well have all the diplomas in the world, but you would amount to nothing in the eyes of nature, unless you manifest the powerful and luminous emanations of a living diploma.

29 November

Whatever faults you may have committed, nothing can stop you from returning to the path of salvation, if that is what you really desire. Tell yourself that heaven has more confidence in a person who has erred and repented than in someone who is blameless. Why? Because someone who has never made a mistake is always liable to do something stupid. They lack experience and are therefore not yet dependable; they can blunder around blindly, sooner or later meeting their downfall. Whereas somebody who has suffered in the devil's clutches will resolve to escape in order to do God's will. Providing they succeed, heaven will be glad of their services, saying, 'At last! Here is someone who we can rely on!'

Of course, that does not mean that you can indulge in all sorts of wild behaviour so that you can better yourself all the more afterwards, no, because it may then take centuries to sort yourself out. Anyway, you have all made quite enough mistakes as it is, so now is the time to learn wisdom and place yourself in the service of heaven.*

* Related reading: *Love and Sexuality (Part I)*, Complete Works Vol. 14, Chap. XI, Part I.

30 November

Lived experiences are always more convincing than explanations.

For example, I go into a house during winter. In order to save on heating, everything is tightly shut and airless, and this close atmosphere has made the inhabitants of the house so muddled that their thoughts and feelings are adversely affected. I could explain to them that this way of life is unhealthy, but I know that my time would be wasted in interminable discussions. Instead, I invite them to come for a fifteen to thirty-minute walk in the fresh air. Then we return to the house and no sooner do we open the door than they exclaim out loud, wondering how they could have put up with such an atmosphere: meaning – because this little story is an allegory – with such stale ideas and stifling philosophies. They understand immediately, without the need for words, because the contrast is obvious. Perhaps they had not quite realized, when they stepped out, how marvellous it is to breathe pure, fresh air, but when they return and suffocate in the stale air, they understand.*

* Related reading: *Freedom, the Spirit Triumphant*, Izvor No. 211, Chap. 5.

1 December

In the dialogue *Symposium*, Plato recounts the myth of the primitive androgyne. In days long gone by, human creatures were said to have lived on earth who were both male and female: they were spherical in shape and had two faces, four arms, four legs, two genital organs, and so forth. These creatures had exceptional vigour and, conscious of their power, they undertook to attack the gods. Greatly concerned, the latter sought a way to weaken them and it was Zeus who found the answer: they would be cut in two! This was done and that is why, ever since then, these two halves of one divided being endlessly roam the world looking for each other in order to unite, and so regain their initial wholeness.

In Plato's myth, one detail is particularly significant: in order to weaken these creatures threatening the power of the gods, Zeus decided to split them in half. The conclusion that emerges from this fact is clear: the power of human beings lies in the possession of both principles. Human beings are akin to gods when they possess both the masculine and feminine principles.*

* Related reading: *The Book of Revelation: a Commentary,* Izvor No. 230, Chap. 3.

2 December

*M*ost human beings are so limited in their love that when a man and woman meet they forget the entire world: nothing else exists as far as they are concerned. They are not yet used to understanding love in a broader sense, so they impoverish and mutilate love. It is no longer divine love that springs forth, showering down upon all creatures.

True love is love that embraces all creatures without limitation, without putting down its roots with just one person. That is why men and women should now be taught to embrace wider concepts, to show less possessiveness and jealousy. The husband should find joy in seeing his wife love the whole world, and the wife should also be happy that her husband has such a big heart. When two truly evolved people get married, they grant each other this mutual freedom beforehand. Each one finds joy in being able to love all creatures in the utmost purity. The wife understands her husband and the husband understands his wife, and they are mutually uplifted, walking together towards heaven, because they are living the true, unlimited life.

3 December

If ancient religions and civilizations have not been able to withstand the test of time and have disappeared, it proves that their values were incapable of creating the new life: they became crystallized, fossilized, and the spirit swept away their old, obsolete forms.

So, do not linger among ruins. Do not look for rubble upon which to found your religion. Many spiritual people seek to return to ancient initiations. That is a mistake. You should not awaken the mysteries of the past because, even from a spiritual point of view, it is dangerous to try to revive what is already dead. Instead of dwelling on the past, reach out to the future, for what your future will be is the present of the higher beings who are watching over you. And so, by receiving what these beings give you, you speed up your evolution.

4 December

*D*o spiritual people carry weight in society? No. Why is that? Because they are not united. Either they ignore each other or they are hostile towards each other. They do not believe they should cooperate together in some way.

On the other hand, look at what materialists undertake and how much they achieve! And scientists – they may be mistaken from an initiatic point of view, they may not have a high ideal or a true overview of things, and may not know the best way to direct their research, but they do work together, they support and help each other. They inform each other of their discoveries, and that is why they have such power in the world. So when will spiritual people decide to unite to work together for the good of humanity?

5 December

Your future will turn out to be what you are building in the present. It is therefore the 'now' that counts. The future is an extension of the present, and the present is nothing other than a consequence, a result of the past. Everything is connected: the past, the present and the future are not separate.

The future will be built on the foundations you are laying today. If these foundations are not good, there is obviously no point in expecting an exceptional future, but if they are good, then there is no need to worry. The roots determine the nature of the trunk, the branches and the fruit. The past is past, but it has brought about the present, and the present forms the roots of the future. So, you are building your future by seeking to improve the present.*

* Related reading: *Freedom, the Spirit Triumphant,* Izvor No. 211, Chap. 3.

6 December

Even if they are not aware of it, people who deny the existence of entities higher than themselves are limiting themselves and sinking into darkness. How do they imagine they will be able to progress and perfect themselves when they do not realize, or refuse to admit that above them exists this sublime hierarchy of angels, archangels, all the way up to the Lord?

Because they cut themselves off from the ascending chain of beings, they have nothing and no one to connect with to receive energies of a higher order and progress along the path of evolution. Of course, they are able to live, to manage materially but, from the spiritual point of view, they stagnate and become mortified. Whereas those who are conscious of the existence of spiritual hierarchies always see this light ahead of them, and are given the impetus to progress.

7 December

*H*ow did the masculine principle (1) create the feminine principle (0), matter? By bending over and joining its two extremities together. At that moment, the circle is formed and the circle represents matter, the universe as a whole. So, 1, the creative principle, comes first in all things, and 0, the creation or the created, must follow. By putting 1 before 0, we increase its power tenfold: 1 becomes 10. But if we do the opposite, 0,1, we reduce its strength and its value ten times.

Let us now transpose this to the inner life. If you put yourself, that which has been created – in other words the 0 – first, and 1, the divine principle, in second place behind you, then you diminish your qualities and your ability to progress. Whereas if you say, 'Lord, only You are truly great, powerful and wise, I will always place You before me in first place and I will follow You', you increase your capabilities: you become 10. This is the attitude of truly spiritual people: they put the Lord first, in order to receive good advice and guidance.*

* Related reading: *Cosmic Balance, the Secret of Polarity,* Izvor No. 237, Chap. 3.

8 December

When children learn to read, they start by identifying the letters of the alphabet. Once they have learnt them well, they are gradually able to recognize them in the words they come across, until one day they can read whole sentences.

Similarly, in the course of their initiation, disciples pass through numerous phases during which they gradually begin to see and make out the letters of the great cosmic book, which are the elements of creation. And when St John writes at the beginning of his Gospel, *'In the beginning was the Word, and the Word was with God, and the Word was God...* All things were made through Him',* it means that in the beginning, all the principles of the divine alphabet came into play: from top to bottom of creation, right to the physical plane, they reproduced the same structures they had created on high. Everything that exists on the physical plane can be considered as words, sentences, poems composed with different elements of the Word.

---

* Related reading: *Angels and other Mysteries of the Tree of Life,* Izvor No. 236, Chap. 7.

9 December

Do you believe that when people say 'I', they really know what they are talking about? When they say, 'I am… ill or in good health, unhappy or happy; I want… money, a car, a wife; I have… such and such a wish, taste, opinion', they really believe they are talking about themselves. That is exactly where they are mistaken. Since they have never analyzed themselves in sufficient depth to know their true nature, they constantly identify themselves with this 'I', which is represented by their physical body, their instincts, their desires, their feelings and their thoughts.

However, if they seek to find their inner self through study and meditation, they will discover that, beyond all appearances, this 'I' they are looking for is an integral part of God Himself. For the truth is that there is no multitude of separate beings, only one single Being who works through all beings, animating them and manifesting within them, even if they are not aware of it. The day they come to feel this reality, humans will draw closer to the divine Source from which they all originate.*

* Related reading: *The Key to the Problems of Existence,* Complete Works Vol. 11, Chap. II.

10 December

If people lack psychology to such an extent that they are unable to understand others, despite their desire to do so, it is because they remain too wrapped up in themselves. It is as if they are blinded by the veil of their own selfish, personal, lower nature, which prevents them from discerning what goes on in the minds or hearts of others.

Even when they love someone, they cannot manage to see through this veil. That is why they are sometimes taken aback by the changes they suddenly see in their wife, husband, children or friends: changes they did not see or feel coming. Only those who can control their lower nature, and are able to forget their own interests, can become good psychologists.

11 December

When it is time to pray and meditate your mind is often elsewhere. And when you need to attend to your work, you often say to yourself, 'Oh, I should meditate. I should spend some time in prayer', and there again you are distracted, so you do your work badly.

Watch yourself and you will see how often your state of mind is not in tune with what you are doing. When you are preparing a meal, doing the washing-up or driving a car, it is not the time to say to yourself, 'Oh, I should do some meditation.' You should be focused on the present in everything you do, because there is a time and a place for everything. Otherwise, you will find that there is no time left for anything as your mind is never in the right place, and you are never, really, anywhere.*

* Related reading: *A New Dawn: Society and Politics in the Light of Initiatic Science (Part II)*, Complete Works Vol. 26, Chap. V.

12 December

The issue of freedom is far from clear in people's minds. Those who believe that being free means to be dependent on nothing and no one do not realize the danger they are in; since their heads and souls are empty, there are gaps everywhere into which all that is negative and dark is ready to rush. They want to be free, yes, but what actually happens is that they end up being totally overwhelmed by other forces of which they know nothing. You see this all too often. The devil finds work for anyone whose mind is not filled with a divine idea: foolishness, extravagances and dangerous adventures, with their trail of consequences. Yes, because they were supposedly 'free'!

We must be committed, filled, occupied, caught up by heaven. Only then are we shielded and truly free. There is no such thing as a vacuum, which is why you must do everything in your power not to be freed from heaven and the light; you must put yourself at the disposal of the celestial forces in order to receive endless blessings. Human beings can find freedom only if they are committed, and submit themselves to heaven.

13 December

Food is made up of particles and energy that come not only from the earth but from the entire cosmos. Yes, elements from the cosmos have materialized in the shape of flowers, vegetables and fruits.

In reality, food materializes on earth exactly in the same way that children materialize in their mother's womb. To begin with, plants and fruits were spirits in space, but as it is impossible to work on the physical plane without a physical body, these spirits had to comply with the laws governing matter in order to be able to act effectively and sustain life here on earth. So they have incarnated, and when we eat, we are coming into contact with living entities.*

* Related reading: *Hrani yoga – The Alchemical and Magical Meaning of Nutrition,* Complete Works Vol. 16, Chap. XI, Part II.

14 December

As they themselves are dishonest, sly and wicked, many people cannot believe that there is such a thing as an honest, sincere and good person. Yes, they judge others according to their own nature and that is why they are always suspicious. Whereas those who are noble and unselfish find it difficult to see wickedness, betrayal or treachery because they also see others according to their own qualities.

Human beings can see only through their own eyes, and what their eyes see is shaped by their own thoughts, feelings, desires and inclinations. If you meet people who talk only about the faults of others, be aware that in fact these faults belong to the speakers themselves; for if they were noble, good, honest and, above all, loving, they would find those same qualities reflected in others too.*

* Related reading: *The Laughter of a Sage,* Izvor No. 243, Chap. 8.

15 December

As soon as you venture into the esoteric sciences you discover magic and, in particular, black magic. But you would do well to stay clear of it, and especially not allow yourselves to be frightened of falling victim to it. If you start to believe you could be affected by black magic, you are already attracting negative currents. Yes, the moment you become weak and vulnerable you attract bad currents and every obscure thing floating in the atmosphere. It is the same with epidemics: if you are weak and receptive, you will catch germs from the people you meet, whereas if you are robust, resistant and emissive, you come through unscathed.

So do not worry about black magic. Strengthen yourselves and think of the light, work with the light and it is this light within you that will repel all that is negative. A wheel spinning fast throws off all dirt, but as soon as it starts to slow down all the dirt sticks to it. The spring that flows vigorously sweeps away the leaves and twigs that could block it. So, instead of giving in to mental laziness, be like the fast flowing spring.*

* Related reading: *The Book of Divine Magic,* Izvor No. 226, Chap. 16.

16 December

You should never forget that human beings are situated at the border of the higher and lower worlds. Christianity expresses this notion with the image of the guardian angel who stands on the right, and the devil who stands on the left. The angel gives good advice and enlightens, whilst the devil seeks to lead astray, and so make human beings its prey. This is a rather simplistic way of putting things, but it corresponds to a certain reality.

This reality is that human beings have two natures: a lower nature and a higher nature. Depending on their degree of evolution, they favour one or the other, and that is how they come into contact with the spirits of darkness or with the spirits of light. Some people say that they do not believe in the entities of the invisible world. Well, whether they believe in them or not is irrelevant: their lower nature and their higher nature are there and it is impossible not to see them in action. It is up to each one of us to decide which influence we will accept.

17 December

Watch what you say very carefully: do not make grand statements, do not commit yourself lightly, because you will provoke the invisible world and you will then have great trouble in keeping your commitments. In fact, you may not even succeed.

A man swears he will never get married. Soon afterwards he meets a woman; she is the least able to make him happy, but he is crazy about her and he marries her. Why? Because there are entities in the invisible world who, seeing this man so sure of himself, want to put him to the test. They tempt him to see what he is capable of, and very soon he succumbs. That is how people often do exactly the opposite of what they so adamantly professed or promised. In some countries, it is the custom for a person to touch wood after saying something. This may seem superstitious, but this gesture says a great deal. It shows that, whilst they are talking, people are conscious of provoking invisible entities, and they touch wood to ward off misfortune.*

---

* Related reading: *Golden Rules for Everyday Life,* Izvor No. 227, Chap. 46.

18 December

As humans, we are linked to beings above us – the angels, the archangels and God Himself, but also to those below us – animals, plants and minerals.

Let us take the example of the two currents circulating in the trunk of a tree. The ascending current carries raw sap to the leaves, where it is transformed into elaborated sap, whilst the descending current takes this elaborated sap to feed the tree. In the Cosmic Tree, man is placed in the path of these two currents, which flow through him, and he must learn to work consciously with them. When he has succeeded in attracting wisdom, light and love from heaven, he passes these qualities on to the beings who are below him and linked to him, right down to the minerals. Then, thanks to another current, these forces ascend from the minerals to the upper realms of creation. Those who consciously bind themselves to this living chain of beings are filled with joy, light and peace.*

* Related reading: *A Philosophy of Universality,* Izvor No. 206, Chap. 6.

19 December

When you wish to find a companion with whom to start a family you have to make an effort to come out of yourself, to be more attentive, more understanding and more generous. However, people make the mistake of failing to understand that they should widen this family circle and extend their love to other creatures and to the whole universe. That is why they are still not happy even though they may have a wife, children, a job and a country to which they belong: because they have not yet managed to widen the circle of their love.

Happiness is loving to infinity, without limiting this love to one person, or two, ten or a hundred... Go on loving those you love, but also love the angels, the archangels, all the celestial hierarchies, the Lord; and in this way your family and friends will find themselves enriched, stronger, purified and made beautiful by all the sublime states you are cherishing in your heart and in your soul. Widen the circle of your love so that you may interact with all the higher creatures, and you will receive inspiration, support and protection.*

* Related reading: *Love and Sexuality (Part II)*, Complete Works Vol. 15, Chap. XXIII.

20 December

Symbolically, the path of the sublimation of the sexual force goes from *Yesod,* passing through *Tiphareth,* to *Kether*. The highest extremity of the central pillar, the holiness of *Kether,* the crowned head, has its origins in the purity of *Yesod,* the sexual organs. The holiness of *Kether* is the sexual energy that disciples endeavour to sublimate, thanks to the powers of *Tiphareth,* until this force can manifest itself higher up, like a golden light above their head.*

Yes, and that is the aim of Initiation: to be able to control a raw force that drags us downwards, make it change direction, and then work on this quintessence until it is transformed into an aura of light.**

* See plate and note on pp. 398 to 401.

** Related reading: *Angels and other Mysteries of the Tree of Life,* Izvor No. 236, Chap. 17.

21 December

The sceptre and the orb are emblems of royalty and, more generally, of power. Each time someone is depicted holding a sceptre in the right hand and an orb in the left, we know that the person must be royal. But what do we know of the deep meaning of these two objects? And do monarchs themselves really know what these objects represent?

The sceptre is usually considered to be the symbol of authority, and the orb the symbol of the territory over which this authority reigns. In reality these symbols have an even greater meaning. The sceptre and the orb represent the two principles: masculine and feminine. The masculine principle is always represented by a straight line – a sceptre, a caduceus, a spear, a sword, a pillar, a tree… and by the right hand. And the feminine principle is represented by a curved line – any hollow or rounded object, a sphere, a vase, a goblet, as well as a chasm, a cave – and by the left hand. Holding the sceptre and the orb signifies that one understands the two principles and knows how to work with them.*

* Related reading: *Cosmic Balance, the Secret of Polarity,* Izvor No. 237, Chap. 11.

22 December

Many people among you are moved by an ideal of justice, honesty or goodness, but they do not know how to act, and continually clash with others, or end up discouraged. So, what should they do? Change their methods.

However noble your ideal may be, do not concern yourself with others, just work at perfecting yourself. That is how, very gradually, whenever you meet people, you will impress them with your light and, as they look at you, it will become clear to them that they are squelching around in mud. Whereas if you try to visit them in their own mud, you will sink into it and get muddy yourself! Work only at becoming luminous and, even if you say nothing, whenever others see you they will understand that it is they themselves who have gone astray.*

* Related reading: *'Know Thyself' – Jnana Yoga (Part II)*, Complete Works Vol. 18, Chap. VIII.

23 December

A gemstone, however small, is a particle of matter capable of holding cosmic forces. But you must not rely on it, thinking that it will protect you, cure you or give you powers; if you do no spiritual work, a gemstone will be of no use to you. A stone is like an antenna and, like an antenna you need to give it a task – messages to transmit. Behind this stone, forces are swirling and vibrating, but it is up to you to give them direction.

Every gemstone has already been prepared by nature to capture certain energies from the cosmos, and to distribute them, propagate them. However, simply possessing a precious stone is not enough to benefit from its virtues. You must learn to use it to undertake specific work on your inner self.*

* Related reading: *The Living Book of Nature,* Izvor No. 216, Chap. 11.

24 December

Life is created through an oscillation between opposing forces or situations. This is a law that applies to all fields. For instance, the abundance and variety of riches on the surface of our planet are due to the fact that this surface is not flat, with many different levels ranging from high summits to the depths of the land and sea. The diversity in climate, flora, fauna, and so on, from which, to some extent, stems the diversity of civilizations, arises from the fact that the surface of the earth is not level and that is wonderful.

Human beings should not be all on the same level either. Why? So there may be a great circulation of fruitful exchanges between them. The one thing they should have in common is a high ideal,* the desire always to go forward in love and in the light. For the rest, let differences remain. It is those differences that make their lives so rich and beautiful.

* Related reading: *What is a Spiritual Master?*, Izvor No. 207, Chap. 9.

25 December

Astrology usually takes only the chart of physical birth into account. But that is not enough, because a person's destiny cannot be determined on the basis of these indications alone. The chart of conception must also be considered, as well as the chart of the second birth, which is the time when the illuminated, renewed person accedes to the divine world, when their consciousness becomes super-consciousness, the consciousness of Christ.

While it is preferable to choose a propitious celestial moment in which to conceive a child on earth, it is not necessary to study astrology to determine the second birth. If people live according to the laws of love, wisdom and purity, that is enough for them to be born a second time, and enter the new life: the kingdom of God.

26 December

The concept of creation is the quintessence of our teaching. Yes, to create, but to create what? Paintings or sculpture? To work on canvas, wood or marble? No, to work on yourself, because you yourself are the true base material.

A sculptor produces a few statues and that is all very well, but when you look at that person, you see that they have never tried to sculpt themselves: they are still merely raw material. No end of people will show you their little paintings, their songs and their poems, and these reflect only their inner chaos. Enough of all these artists! Where are the true artists, ready to start the real work, ready to sculpt their inner selves? This kind of work is unknown, it is unheard of, but it is the work of the future.*

* Related reading: *Youth: Creators of the Future,* Izvor No. 233, Chap. 17.

Jesus said to his disciples in the Gethsemane, *'Stay awake, and pray'*, Christians throughout history have taken this to be a directive for everyday life. So the poor things have woken themselves up in the middle of the night to say their prayers, fighting tiredness and disrupting their body's natural rhythms. We need sleep to allow our bodies to rest. It is not so much on the physical plane that we should stay awake – 'stay awake' is above all a precept for the spiritual plane.

To 'stay awake' or keep watch means to connect through thought to the One within us who never sleeps – this is whom we must reach. This eternal Watcher dwells between our two eyebrows. He sees everything, he records everything, he understands everything. Only when we succeed in uniting with him can we properly comply with the precept of Jesus: 'Stay awake'.*

* Related reading: *The True Meaning of Christ's Teaching,* Izvor No. 215, Chap. 9.

28 December

*T*he caduceus of Hermes is a representation of the structure of man: the two serpents intertwined around the central staff are the two negative and positive currents that wind around either side of the spine. The Hindus call them Ida and Pingala, and they call the central channel inside the spine Sushumna. An Initiate is a person who knows how to work with both currents. As their work progresses, they acquire powers that allow them to act on nature, on themselves and on others. That is why the caduceus has become the symbol of medicine.

The caduceus of Hermes represents a whole philosophy and discipline of life. It teaches us how to work with the two negative and positive currents that circulate in the universe. A true Initiate, who works with the two principles, who knows the power of the two principles as an instrument, a weapon, a medicine – this Initiate possesses true powers.*

* Related reading: *Cosmic Balance, the Secret of Polarity*, Izvor No. 237, Chap. 9.

29 December

*E*very time we win over temptation put before us by our lower nature, we acquire new strength. What is difficult of course is to maintain this state of grace. As long as we live on earth, we cannot remain for long on the heights we have managed to reach. We must continue to struggle, over and over, to conquer them again. When we leave the physical world for the spiritual world, we will no longer need to struggle because we will no longer be subject to temptation. But as long as we remain on earth, we must work up to the very last minute. It is the same when it comes to eating and breathing: we ate yesterday but we must also eat today and we will have to eat again tomorrow. We have just taken a breath and right away, we must start over again.

One experience has led us to understand the meaning of life, but if we do not want to lose this meaning, we must have another experience, and then another, and another. We have overcome temptation? We will be tempted again, and once again, we will have to try to win the battle.*

* Related reading: *The Powers of Thought,* Izvor No. 224, Chap. 8.

30 December

*T*he soul is hungry and the spirit is thirsty. The soul eats fire and the spirit drinks light. The spirit is a masculine principle, the soul a feminine principle, and they each nourish themselves with the complementary element. The soul – which aspires to a positive, active and dynamic principle – eats fire, whereas the spirit – which is masculine – needs to be nourished by the feminine principle, and so drinks light.

And just as the masculine principle begets the feminine principle, fire begets light. Light is a manifestation, an emanation of fire. When you light a fire it produces light. And the purer the materials that feed this fire, the more subtle and bright is the light.*

* Related reading: *Light is a Living Spirit,* Izvor No. 212, Chap. 1.

31 December

Do you feel the harmony we create all together when we sing? Tomorrow a new year begins, and tonight we can say we have sung for the year that is leaving. The old year is very pleased because we are seeing it out with a lot of love.

As for the New Year, we can already start to prepare it consciously this evening by setting ourselves a goal: a quality to be developed, a bad habit to beat, or a project to realize for the glory of God. By focusing on this thought, this wish, it is as if you are laying the foundation stone, and then all the luminous spirits of nature will come to your aid and help you accomplish your divine project. That is what you should be concentrating on at the end of the year. Unfortunately, not many people do. Most are getting ready to indulge in all kinds of excess. It is hardly surprising if the year then turns out badly for them. So you, who are disciples of the divine school, endeavour to receive the New Year within you by placing yourselves under the sign of light.*

* Related reading: *The New Year,* Brochure, No. 301.

The Night of Wesak

*E*ach year, in the Himalayas, during the night of the full moon in May, the ceremony of Wesak takes place.*

The full moon in May is doubly under the influence of Taurus: the sun has been in this sign since 21 April, and the moon is also exalted in this sign.** Taurus represents prolific nature, fertility and abundance, emphasized further by the fact that it is the home of Venus, the planet of creation. So the full moon in May offers the best conditions for working with the forces of nature to attract heaven's blessings for the harvest and livestock, but also for human beings. For, if humans know how to attract the beneficial effects circulating through the cosmos at this time, they too can benefit from them, not only on the physical plane but also on the spiritual plane. This is why, by means of meditations, prayers, chants and magical invocations, initiates seek to create lines of force in space that will attract energies, which they send to all beings who are vigilant, awakened and capable of participating at this event.

* Wesak is the festival of the Buddha. In Tibet, it is celebrated in the valley of Wesak.

** Some years, when the sun is in Taurus, the full moon takes place in April.

There are places on earth that are more favourable than others for this cosmic work. The site where the ceremony of Wesak takes place is the most powerful of all. Some initiates go there physically, others by astral projection. But it is possible for everyone, including you, to take part in thought. During this night, you must not keep any metal object on you, since metal is not a good conductor of the waves of energy that come down from spiritual regions. But the only truly essential condition for being admitted to this festival is harmony. So be careful not to hold onto any negative thought or feeling towards others, and find the right inner attitude that will allow you to receive the blessings that the initiates send to the children of God on this night.

INDEX

A

Acts – they provide more joy than thoughts and feelings do, 25 April

Adaptability – knowing how to adapt without abandoning one's ideal, 17 July

Adversaries – how to consider them in order to evolve, 07 April

Alpha and omega – living letters of creation, 12 June

Ambiance – it brings out people's good or bad side, 03 April

Anarchy – we will be the victims of the resulting disorder, 06 Nov.

Angels of the four elements – contained in food, 22 Feb.

Archangel Gabriel – presides over the region of Yesod, 25 March

Archangel Michael – we should link ourselves to him and ask him to protect us, 29 Sept.

Art
- artists must create works that inspire the human soul, 21 June
- true creation is to sculpt our inner selves, 26 Dec.

Artists – those who have destroyed their own masterpieces have harmed themselves, 23 Nov.

Astrology – birth chart, chart of conception and chart of the second birth, 25 Dec.

Attention – self-awareness of our inner realm, 19 Nov.

Attitude – adopting the right attitude towards the Creator to receive His blessings, 15 June

Attraction and repulsion – they are never reliable guides, 26 Jan.

Aura
- work on it to attract every blessing, 07 Jan.
- its colours are nourished and maintained by the virtues, 09 June

- the practice of divine virtues attracts the corresponding colours, 15 July
- its colours are a pass to enter the regions to which they correspond, 20 Nov.

Autumn equinox – presided over by Archangel Michael, 22 Sept.

B

Beauty – seize hold of inner beauty in order to find it on the outside, 29 July

Black magic – fear of it attracts it, the light repels it, 15 Dec.

Blessings from heaven – to obtain them give something in exchange, 12 July

Body –physical symmetry and psychic polarization, 15 April

Breathing
- everything in nature breathes, even the earth itself, 27 Feb.
- the importance of finding the appropriate rhythm, 17 Oct.

C

Caduceus of Hermes – representation of two currents, positive and negative, 28 Dec.

Cardinal feasts – participate in their work through our consciousness, 31 March

Child – help the wilful child to channel their energies, 28 Aug.

Choir – the effects of singing all together in harmony, 23 July

Church – it must refine the forms so that they may express the spirit better, 16 Oct.

Circle with the central point – matter animated by the spirit, 25 Oct.

Clairvoyants – there are others ways to know your future, 29 April

Communion
- the source of true knowledge, 09 Jan.
- with the Creator in all the acts of everyday life, 10 Sept.

Competing – rising on the spiritual plane just as on the social ladder, 05 Sept.

Consciousness
- seek to identify your desires, feelings and thoughts, 19 June
- of minerals, plants, animals and human beings, 16 July

Consecrating an object – begin by exorcizing it, 06 March

Cosmic Tree – binding ourselves to the living chain of beings, 18 Dec.

Creation – the perpetual movement of the scales, 06 April

Criticism – redouble your efforts so as not to dampen your enthusiasm, 19 Sept.

Cross – it expresses a cosmic reality, 29 March

D

The **desire** to become a conductor of light must come from the person himself, 08 Nov.

Desires, needs and inclinations – they determine a person's destiny, 13 July

Destiny – our afterlife is determined by our aspirations on earth, 11 Oct.

Devil – he possesses only the power that we give him, 20 March

Difficulties
- overcome them by keeping your thoughts focused on the divine world, 12 Jan.
- do not take them too seriously, 11 March

Diploma – not a piece of paper, but one printed on your face and body, 28 Nov.

Disciple – the attitude to adopt when we are praised or insulted, 21 Nov.

Discontent – a harmful habit that makes us unattractive to others, 18 Feb.

Discouragement – to avoid it, work at perfecting yourself, 22 Dec.

Diversity among human beings – makes life rich and beautiful, 24 Dec.

Divine idea – an entity that regenerates and restores us, 21 July

Divine laws – we cannot transgress them with impunity, 22 Jan.

Divine philosophy – study it and apply it, 06 Feb.

Doctors – they can have a beneficial influence on their patients, 16 March

E

Economic interests – they must not be a society's prime concern, 25 Aug.

Education
- the way in which we speak to children is very important, 02 Oct.
- teach children to establish a connection with heaven, 03 Nov.

Emotions – negative or positive, they influence our health, 21 Feb.

Entities of darkness – we need to protect ourselves against them, 02 Feb.

Eve – the importance of the last moment before going to sleep, 24 Nov.

Evening prayer before bedtime – story about the monk who drank, 04 Aug.

Evil
- transform it through the secret of unity, 17 Feb.
- it cannot enter a person who is occupied by the Lord, 06 Aug.
- it is driven out of the sublime regions, 08 Oct.
- do not fight it head-on; strengthen yourself in order to resist better and take better action, 29 Oct.

Evolution – take into account the experience of others, 16 Feb.

Exercise and formula – to become alive and vibrant, 20 July

Experiences – they are more convincing than explanations, 30 Nov.

F

Face and body – sculpted by our thoughts and feelings, 11 Nov.

Faith is not enough – it must be accompanied by the corresponding actions and efforts, 13 Oct.

Fate – one's destiny can be changed by the spirit within us, 05 Jan.

Fear – vanquished by love and knowledge, 06 May

Feast of St John – inner fire symbolized by the dragon, 24 June

Feet – they have spiritual centres to be developed, 05 March

Fidelity – in order to achieve it, first we must love it, 03 Feb.

Fire and water – man and woman, the conditions for creating life, 06 Oct.

Flame – a symbol of the spirit that we must nourish for it to become powerful, 28 Oct.

Food
- subtle beings nourish themselves with light, colours and sounds, 14 July
- living entities that come from the entire cosmos, 13 Dec.

Forgetting oneself – in order to think of one's partner, one's children, 03 Aug.

Forms must change – only the principles are eternal, 03 Oct.

Freedom
- it does not exist in the absence of submission to God, 21 Jan.
- doing the will of God in order to win it, 26 May
- efforts to be spiritually free, 14 June
- possible only if we submit ourselves to heaven, 12 Dec.

Fulfilment – found in brotherly, collective life, 16 Jan.

G

Gemstones – use them to undertake work on your inner self, 23 Dec.

Geometric figures – they symbolize the truth very simply, 27 Oct.

Give instead of taking – the law of love, 20 Jan.

Give thanks for what you have and for what you do not have, 25 July

God
- whether He exists or not depends on our state of awareness, 18 April
- the evolution of his image towards a God of love, 13 May
- by cutting our ties with Him, we lose light and vitality, 24 May
- both masculine and feminine, 23 Oct.
- animates all beings, works and manifests within them, 09 Dec.

God, our Father – we are in Him and He is in us, 21 May

God drew a circle and limited Himself in order to create the world, 15 Oct.

God in the book of Exodus – "I will be who I will be", 29 June

Good and evil – we can never really make valid judgments on them, 23 April

Gratitude
- give something in exchange for everything we receive, 11 April
- do not forget to thank the Lord, 12 Nov.

Greeting and embracing each other – always do so with love, 26 March

Guardian angel – attracting its blessings by thinking of the child, 10 April

Guide – we also need one for our inner life, 06 July

H

Hand
- our five fingers correspond to the five cardinal virtues, 18 Jan.
- each finger picks up and transmits waves, 27 May

Happiness
- it can present itself to you in different forms, 24 Jan.
- base it on heaven's approval rather on that of humans, 05 Feb.
- to be happy, open yourself up to others, 30 May
- true happiness lies in the possessions of the soul and the spirit, 04 Oct.

- widen the circle of your love, love to infinity, 19 Dec.

Harm – the harm that we do to ourselves is reflected on the whole world, 17 Nov.

Harmony – creating it when we sing together, 31 Dec.

Health
- free the flow of energies by means of pure thoughts, 09 Feb.
- as with food, properly chew the sun's rays, 02 April

Heavenly bank – building credit through our acts of selflessness, 18 July

Heavenly inspiration – distinguishing it from mystical delirium, 08 April

Higher or lower nature – favouring one or the other, 16 Dec.

Hooks – listen to the sages in order to recognize them and escape them, 13 Sept.

Horse – it represents our lower nature, and we must hold the reins, 27 Nov.

House – make a promise when asking for it to be protected, 22 July

Human beings
- placed between the lower world and the higher world, 27 Jan.
- knowing ourselves through matter, 01 March

Hygiene (physical and psychic) – reducing waste, 27 June

I

'I am He' – the meaning of this formula from the sages of India, 28 Feb.

Ideal
- always add a spiritual element to your life, 29 Feb.
- without a spiritual ideal, your life will be in disarray, 18 Aug.

Illness – ridding ourselves of accumulated wastes, 07 Sept.

Illumination – fleeting, up until the day the light no longer leaves us, 01 Oct.

Improving ourselves – our efforts are the only thing that counts for heaven, 08 Jan.

Impulsiveness – it is vital to learn to control ourselves, 23 June

Independence –we are always influenced, 09 May

Inheritance – the Lord does not show it to us right away, 02 July

Initiates
- they exchange with human beings in the same way the sun exchanges with the earth, 01 May
- they put the outer world at the service of the inner world, 17 Sept.
- nourish themselves with the divine life that human beings carry within them, 07 Nov.

Initiatic Science – its universal criterion: work for the kingdom of God, 21 April

Initiatic tale – the symbol of the knight, his shield and his sword, 11 Feb.

Initiatic Teaching – do not abandon it, 11 Jan.

Initiation
- a very long path before being able to guide others, 23 Sept.
- learning the letters of the great cosmic book, 08 Dec.
- its aim is to endeavour to sublimate sexual energy, 20 Dec.

Initiations of Antiquity – do not return to them, reach out to the future, 03 Dec.

Inner states – be vigilant about them to avoid being engulfed, 11 May

Inner sun – from which we can draw everything we need, 08 Sept.

Inner world – reinforce it, enrich it in order to stay safe, 14 Sept.

Intellect – do not listen to its reasoning, but rather to your intuition, 03 March

Intuition
- it is akin to both the intellect and the heart, 30 March
- superior to clairvoyance, 10 Aug.

- it can be developed only through a pure life, 29 Aug.

Isis unveiled – the Mysteries in the temples of Antiquity, 04 July

J

Jesus
- "My Father and I are one", 15 Jan.
- he gave depth and breadth to the religion of his forebears, 13 Feb.
- "The kingdom of God is at hand": three statements, 12 Oct.

Joy – in order to hold on to it learn to share it by means of thought, 02 Jan.

Judging – we can see others only through our own eyes, 14 Dec.

K

Karma – instil a little more kindness and purity into your actions so as not to be subject to it, 14 Feb.

Keep watch – on the spiritual plane, uniting with the eternal Watcher, 27 Dec.

King
- the symbols of the sceptre and the orb held in his hands, 30 Jan.
- the sceptre and the globe, the masculine and feminine principles, 21 Dec.

Kingdom of God and His Justice – a goal to pursue, 31 July

Knowledge – cultivate love and willpower rather than book learning, 07 Feb.

Knowledge of people's true nature – so as not to have any illusions, 04 May

Knowledge that you put into practice will remain yours, 20 June

L

Law of the jungle – it may rule on earth but not in heaven, 28 July

Laws governing the three categories of human beings, 27 Sept.

Level of consciousness – it determines destiny, 28 May

Life
- an instinctive and disorderly life leads to irreparable losses, 20 Feb.
- like a ball that we must inflate with air: faith, hope and love, 01 July

Light
- the food of the future for human beings, 19 Feb.
- the most essential element we can give, 15 Aug.
- it will enter your mind only when you open the curtains, 10 Oct.
- the most perfect of all God's creatures for nothing can match its speed, 21 Oct.

Light and darkness – two forces that nature uses for its work, 07 Aug.

Limitation and expansion – both are necessary, 14 Aug.

Links – thoughts and feelings are ties, threads, 18 June

The **Lord** – imposing your will on Him by fighting with the arms of love, 17 June

Love
- its vibrations can influence objects, 29 Jan.
- prolonging its subtle manifestations, 09 March
- only an immense, rich and pure love brings happiness, 26 June
- even people who are difficult to bear, 09 Aug.
- do not be in a hurry to declare your love, 18 Oct.
- understanding it in a broader, more universal, divine sense, 02 Dec.

Love or friendship – win them only by means of light, 01 Aug.

Love without waiting to be loved and you will be free, 18 March

Lyre of Orpheus – the 7 strings, a symbol of man, 04 Jan.

M

Magic – everyone unconsciously practises black or white magic, 12 March

Magic wand – an instrument that links heaven and earth, 15 May

Marriage – the true blessing is love itself, 07 July

Masculine principle – put the Lord in first place, 07 Dec.

Mass – communion requires both the wine and the bread, 28 March

Master
- his approach towards human beings in view of helping them, 28 April
- a being who has total control of his thoughts, feelings and actions, 25 Sept.

Master's goal – training workers who will spread the light, 14 Oct.

Matter
- make use of everything, but towards a divine goal, 22 April
- it limits us, obliging us to undertake special work, 13 June
- it is actually condensed light, 07 Oct.

Measure in all things – even the measure of goodness, 11 Aug.

Meditate
- for both oneself and for the collectivity, 15 March
- to purify and illuminate everything about us, 05 April

Meditating
- begin by controlling your thoughts and feelings, 22 Aug.
- first get rid of your negative states, 03 Sept.
- calm your lower astral and mental bodies and let your mind soar, 10 Nov.

Meditation
- first get rid of your old clothing, 19 July
- being present and focused in everything that we do, 11 Dec.

Mentalities – transforming them in order to change the world, 04 March

Mercury – symbols of the moon and the sun, water and fire, 22 May

Mistakes – they must not stop us from returning to the path of salvation, 29 Nov.

Money – great strength is needed to resist its temptations, 09 July

Money to help others – strengthen yourself spiritually first, 03 July

Morality – based on the science of cause and consequence, 20 Aug.

Music of the Spheres – harmony between all the elements, 05 June

N

Nature

- how to repay it for everything it gives us, 09 April
- inhabited by spirits with whom we can communicate, 30 April
- by greeting it each morning, you will gradually feel something harmonizing within you, 24 Sept.
- learn to recognize its etheric body and beyond, 26 Sept.
- look upon it with a sense of sacredness, 30 Aug.

New Year – wishes for all the blessings of heaven, 01 Jan.

Nudity – expresses either spiritual poverty or spiritual wealth, 28 June

Number 2 – the 1 divided into positive and negative, 26 Aug.

Nutrition –consider it to be a cosmic process, 24 March

O

Obstacles – rough edges that enable us to climb towards the light, 22 June

Occult sciences – erudition and true knowledge, 08 March

Occult sciences and Initiatic Science – the difference, 12 May

Opening ourselves to the positive influences around us, 24 Aug.

Opinion – ask for heaven's opinion when you need guidance, 14 Jan.

Organization – integral to the notion of harmony, 11 July

Organs – the materialization of energies, currents and forces, 16 June

Osiris – a black god because he is the light beyond all light, 02 June

Others – think of them for your own pleasure, just as the sun does, 04 Sept.

P

Peace
- it is from within ourselves that we must remove the causes of war, 17 March
- savouring it by putting a stop to all our little sorrows, 27 July

Pedagogy – most noble, most meaningful profession, 26 Nov.

People with responsibilities must raise themselves up to a higher viewpoint, 16 Sept.

Perfume – Eve exhaled an exquisite scent in Paradise, 31 May

Place – respective place of the masculine and the feminine, 31 Aug.

Pleasures – direct and control them by exercising wisdom, 05 July

Poetry – greeting the visible and invisible creatures in the morning, 24 Oct.

Power – human beings' power lies in possessing both principles, 01 Dec.

Prayer – to call on the help of the angels of the four elements, 28 Sept.

Prayer and meditation – their usefulness for the whole world, 28 Jan.

Precious stones – they reflect the beauty of the divine world, 05 Aug.

Present – the result of the past, the roots of the future, 05 Dec.

Pride makes human beings poor; humility brings them wealth, 14 March

Principles (the 2) – the masculine principal and the feminine principal are equally important, 26 April

Problems – they could be solved in twenty-four hours, 18 Sept.

Profession – guiding others towards the light is the most difficult of all, 14 April

Progressing – recognizing the existence of higher entities above us, 06 Dec.

Promises – do not make them lightly, 17 Dec.

Protection – against evil entities, 20 April

Psychic life – defending it through vigilance and exercises, 25 Jan.

Psychology – forgetting our own interests so as to understand others, 10 Dec.

Purification – either through hardship or by means of the spiritual sun, 23 March

Purity
- determined by the intention, and not by the action, 19 March
- the foundation of the spiritual life, which bears the weight of the edifice, 06 June
- to become more lucid, healthier and joyful, 07 June

Purity of our blood, thoughts and feelings – our best defence against illness, 25 May

Q

Qualities – the role of the sun in obtaining them over time, 19 Aug.

R

Real change – become a wellspring, a sun, 07 March

Receptivity to the invisible world – remain vigilant and active, 16 Nov.

Reciprocity – giving in order to receive, 10 June

Recognition – recognizing the beings we have loved in the next world, 23 Jan.

Relations with others – see their good side, 27 March

Religion – it has not succeeded in developing our spiritual centres, 13 April

Renouncement – abstaining from baser pleasures in order to fuel the spirit, 02 Aug.

Rose petal – a channel that can put us in contact with the qualities of Venus, 16 May

Rosy cross – it symbolizes an initiate, a perfect human being, 23 Feb.

S

Sacrifices – those made for a sublime idea transform everything into gold, 22 March

Saturn – represents time and eternity, 10 Feb.

Seeing on the spiritual plane – it is up to us to project rays of light, 12 Aug.

Self-control – to master feelings and thoughts, start by controlling your hands, 16 April

Self-mastery – begin by mastering your thoughts, 06 Jan.

Selfishness – it is not a good solution for anyone, 04 April

Sensitivity and touchiness – openness or a closed door to the divine world, 26 Oct.

Sephirotic tree – the best guide for our spiritual work, 14 Nov.

Sewing or embroidery – they tell the whole story of life, 06 Sept.

Sex – psychically, human beings possess both the masculine and the feminine principles, 23 Aug.

Sexuality – learning the right way to regard each other, 24 Feb.

Silence – a condition for the most luminous creations, 10 Jan.

Simplicity of a diamond – unify our thoughts and desires, 24 April

Singing and praying – powers that dispel the darkness, 08 June

Situations – avoid seeing only the negative, bad side, 22 Oct.

Skin – it can distil a fragrance similar to that of flowers, 31 May

Sleep

- always go to sleep with a good thought in your head, 29 May
- go to sleep with a light-filled thought, a feeling of love, 25 Nov.

Snowdrop – its strength and power reside in its love, 04 Feb.

Social inequalities – linked to past incarnations, 30 July

Soul – each body possesses a soul, 13 Aug.

Soul and spirit – the soul eats fire, the spirit drinks light, 30 Dec.

Spirit and matter – human beings must reach up towards the spirit, 09 Sept.

Spirit of Christ – making contact with it by means of our spirit, 19 May

Spirits of darkness – very wily with their promises, 10 July

Spiritual knowledge – use it only to help others, 16 Aug.

Spiritual life

- keeping ourselves free for work of a heavenly nature, 25 Feb.
- certain unpleasant effects at first, 01 June

Spiritual Master – he looks after his disciples night and day, 08 July

Spiritual Masters – they help us with our inner life, 02 Sept.

Spiritual maturity – to be truly an adult, 10 March

Spiritual people – they must unite to work for the good of humanity, 04 Dec.

Spiritual work

- our inner achievements are invisible, 19 Oct.
- draw a circle of light around yourself, 30 Oct.

Spiritualist or materialist? – It depends on your level of consciousness, 20 Sept.

Spirituality – comparable to the action of the sun on the earth, 21 March

Spring – like a spring, the love that pours forth rejects impurities, 15 Feb.

Standards – the need for references in our spiritual life, 31 Jan.

Stars – contemplating them puts our problems and worries into perspective, 18 Nov.

Strength in unity – a motto that applies to every human being, 31 Oct.

Subconscious – it records every single event, 12 Feb.

Success – it depends on our ability to see, to observe, 08 May

Suffering – it affects only matter that is not absolutely pure, 22 Nov.

Suicide – it is paid for with suffering in the afterlife, 26 July

Summit – focus on the summit to see the truth, 03 Jan.

Sun
- For millions of years, it continues to shine and give its blessings, 01 April.
- an unrivalled model of perfection, the true religion, 03 May
- a dazzling world inhabited by the most highly evolved entities, 24 July

Sunrise – linking ourselves with the spirit of Christ, the solar Spirit, 13 Nov.

T

Take stock of your life regularly – sort through your activities, keep only what is essential, 01 Nov.

Tastes and tendencies – do not make them your guiding principle, 02 Nov.

Technical progress – it must be given a different direction, towards the spirit, 05 Nov.

Temptation – each time we overcome it, we acquire new strength, 29 Dec.

Third eye – it warns us of dangers and obstacles, 12 April

Thought
-put it in first place, before feelings, 27 April
- the best gift that God has given us, 02 May

Three worlds – that of facts, of laws and of principles, 13 Jan.

Three worlds (the) – the body, the soul and the spirit, 17 April

Tiredness – you must take a step and do something to chase it away, 17 Aug.

To know, will, dare and keep silent – precept of the Initiates, 09 Nov.

Tolstoy – tale of the king and the seed the size of a hen's egg, 08 Aug.

Traces of the Initiates on earth – their spirit is in the sun, 03 June

Tree – meditate on the contrast between its lower and upper parts, 05 May

Tree of the Knowledge of Good and Evil, 14 May

Trials
- their positive side, 02 March
- to get through them, work for the coming of the kingdom of God, 21 Sept.

Trials and difficulties – the story of a grain of wheat, 15 Nov.

True life – seeking to be the king of ourselves, 09 Oct.

Truth
- Jesus said, 'Know the truth, and the truth will make you free', 19 April
- study it by linking beings and things with life, 10 May
- those who live in truth stand out by reason of their kindness and altruism, 17 May
- it is not enough to believe, we must study, verify, 20 Oct.

Truths – repeat them often in order to triumph, 15 Sept.

U

Umbilical cord – with the mother, with the nature, with God, 25 June

Unity
- human beings share the same essential needs, 23 May
- the condition for happiness, success and health, 11 June

Unity and duality – in reality all human beings are one, 30 Sept.

Universe
- comparison with a tree, from the roots to the fruit, 30 June
- created by God by projecting light, 01 Sept.

V

Veil of Isis – lifting it to pierce the mysteries of nature, 20 May
Vigilance – indispensable to protect our good impulses, 07 May
Voice – put it in the service of the forces of light, 05 Oct.
Voice of silence – the expression of true life, 12 Sept.

W

Waste – rejecting physical and psychic waste in order to purify ourselves, 04 Nov.

Water – its four states: solid, liquid, gaseous and etheric, 04 June

Wealth of the spirit – you have to love and understand it, 17 Jan.

Willpower is not enough – we need heavenly protection to resist our baser tendencies, 13 March

Wisdom and love – the small hand and the big hand of a clock, 27 Aug.

Women
- they must work on their inner beauty, 01 Feb.
- dominated by men, compensation, 31 Aug.

Words
- intermediaries between pure thought and physical realization, 26 Feb.
- often used to provoke certain reactions, 18 May
- speak with love to nature and to human beings, 21 Aug.

Work with thought – the most important work for your future, 11 Sept.

Worries, pain – call on thought, which knows how to remedy everything, 08 Feb.

Y

Yogas – they all share the same goal, which is to help us draw closer to the truth, 19 Jan.

Note: The three fundamental activities which characterize human beings are thinking (by means of the intellect or mind), feeling (by means of the heart), and doing (by means of the physical body). You must not believe that only the physical body is material; the heart and mind are also material instruments, but the matter of which they are made is far subtler than that of the physical body.

HIGHER NATURE

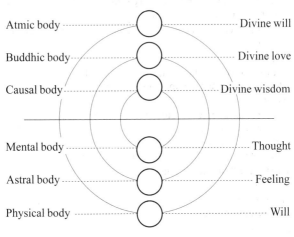

Atmic body	Divine will
Buddhic body	Divine love
Causal body	Divine wisdom
Mental body	Thought
Astral body	Feeling
Physical body	Will

LOWER NATURE

An age-old esoteric tradition teaches that the support or vehicle of feeling is the astral body, and that of the intellect, the mental body. But this trinity made up of our physical, astral, and mental bodies, constitutes our imperfect human nature, and the three faculties of thought, feeling, and action also exist on a higher level, their vehicles being respectively, the causal, buddhic, and atmic bodies which go to make up our divine self.

In the diagram, the three large concentric circles indicate the links which exist between the lower and the higher bodies. The physical body, which represents strength, will, and power on the material level, is linked to the atmic body, which represents divine power, strength, and will. The astral body, which represents our egotistical, personal feelings and desires, is linked to the buddhic body, which represents divine love. The mental body, which represents our ordinary, self-serving thoughts, is linked to the causal body, which represents divine wisdom.

(Man's Psychic Life: Elements and Structures,
Izvor Collection No. 222, chap. 3)

Introduction to the Sephirotic Tree

Jesus said, 'And this is eternal life, that they may know you, the only true God'.

For those who aspire to know the Creator of heaven and earth, to feel his presence, to enter into his infinity and his eternity, it is necessary to have a deep understanding of a system that explains the world. The system that seemed to me to be the best, the most extensive and at the same time the most precise I found in the cabbalistic tradition – the sephirotic Tree, the Tree of Life. Its knowledge offers the deepest, most structured, overall view of what we need to study and work on.

The cabbalists divide the universe into ten regions or ten sephiroth corresponding to the first ten numbers (the word 'sephirah' and its plural 'sephiroth' mean enumeration). Each sephirah is identified by means of five names: the name of God, the name of the sephirah, the name of the archangel at the head of the angelic order, the angelic order itself, and a planet. God directs these ten regions, but under a different name in each one. This is why the Cabbalah gives God ten names, each corresponding to different attributes. God is one, but manifests in a different way in each region.

This Tree of Life is presented as a very simple diagram, but its contents are inexhaustible. For me it is the key that allows the mysteries of creation to be deciphered. It is not meant to teach us astronomy or cosmology, and anyway no one can say exactly what the universe is or how it was created. This Tree represents an explanatory system of the world that is by nature mystical. Through meditation and contemplation and a life of saintliness, the exceptional minds that devised it came to grasp a cosmic reality, and it is essentially their teaching that survives to this day, passed down by tradition and continually taken up and meditated on through the centuries.

A spiritual Master is conscious of the responsibilities he is taking by allowing humans to enter this holy sanctuary, and so when you approach this knowledge you must do so with much humility, respect and reverence. By returning often to this diagram, you will find lights being switched on inside you. You will certainly never manage to explore all its riches, but from Malkuth to Kether this representation of an ideal world will always draw you higher.

TREE OF LIFE

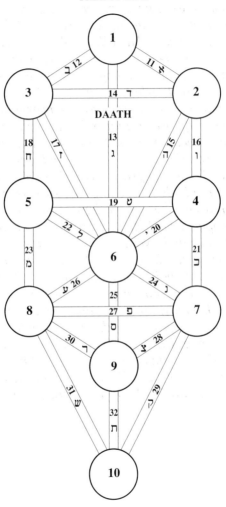

TREE OF LIFE

1 Ehieh
Kether – *Crown*
Metatron
Hayoth haKades ch – *Seraphim*
Rashith haGalgalim – *First Swirlings (Neptune)*
♆

3 Jehovah
Binah – *Understanding*
Tzaphkiel
Aralim – *Thrones*
Shabbathai – *Saturn*
♄

2 Yah
Chokmah – *Wisdom*
Raziel
Ophanim – *Cherubim*
Mazloth – *The Zodiac (Uranus)*
♅

5 Elohim Gibor
Geburah – *Severity*
Kamaël
Seraphim – *Powers*
Maadim – *Mars*
♂

4 El
Chesed – *Mercy*
Tzsadkiel
Hashmalim – *Dominations*
Tzedek– *Jupiter*
♃

6 Eloha vaDaath
Tiphareth – *Beauty*
Mikhaël
Malakhim – *Virtues*
Shemesh – *Sun*
☉

8 Elohim Tzebaoth
Hod – *Glory*A
Raphaël
Bnei-Elohim – *Archangels*
Kokab – *Mercury*
☿

7 Jehovah Tzebaoth
Netzach – *Victory*
Haniel
Elohim – *Principalities*
Noga – *Venus*
♀

9 Shaddai El Hai
Yesod – *Foundation*
Gabriel
Kerubim – *Angels*
Levana – *Moon*
☽

10 Adonai-Melek
Malkuth – *The Kingdom*
Uriel (Sandalfon)
Ishim – *Beatified Souls*
Olem Ha Yesodoth – *Earth*
♁

Worldwide Editor and Distributor

Editions Prosveta (France)

www.prosveta.fr • www.prosveta.com • contact@prosveta.fr

Tel. +33 4 94 19 33 33

For an updated list, please visit
www.prosveta.fr

English Distributors

AUSTRALIA
Prosveta Australia • prosveta.au@aapt.net.au
CANADA
Prosveta • www.prosveta-canada.com • prosveta@prosveta-canada.com
FRANCE
Editions Prosveta • www.prosveta.fr • international@prosveta.com
IRELAND
Prosveta UK • www.prosveta.co.uk • orders@prosveta.co.uk
LEBANON
Prosveta Liban • www.prosveta-liban.com • prosveta_lb@terra.net.lb
NETHERLANDS
Stichting Prosveta Nederland • www.prosveta.nl • vermeulen@prosveta.nl
NEW ZEALAND
Prosveta New Zealand • www.oma-books.co.nz
johnson.susan34@gmail.com
NORWAY
Prosveta Norden • www.prosveta.no • info@prosveta.no
UNITED KINGDOM
Prosveta UK • www.prosveta.co.uk • orders@prosveta.co.uk
UNITED STATES OF AMERICA
Wellsprings of Life • www.prosveta-usa.com • wellspringsoflife@mail.com
Prosveta Books • www.prosvetabooks.com • prosvetausa@gmail.com

Editions Prosveta owns the worldwide copyright of the work of Master Omraam Mikhaël Aïvanhov, publishes in French and in English, and grants translation and editorial or joint-editorial rights to other languages. Those who have a licence to use the Prosveta® brand are independent and not affiliated with Editions Prosveta nor to each other.

———————

Printed in June 2023
by MultiPrint
Sofia – Bulgaria
———
Dépôt légal: juin 2023